FORWAI

D0554958

THE PAIN OF KNOWLEDGE.
AN INVITATION TO BRING THE PAIN.

"Whoever loves discipline loves
knowledge, but whoever hates correction
is stupid."

Proverbs 12:1

···

This book is written to challenge your fundamental notions regarding God, the trinity, and your spiritual purpose on this earth. This is not a book intended to make you comfortable and feel good. It is intended to push your basic beliefs so far that they actually begin to change. If successful, it should change how you see your heavenly father and how you approach him and his will. This book will make you responsible for new knowledge and the actions that knowledge should guide you to. With that in mind this forward will not discuss the book but will prepare you for the onus you take on by reading it.

RESPONSIBILITY

This really can't be expressed better than it was in Spiderman. With great power comes great responsibility. It really holds true in all facets of our life.

The guy who worked at your office for years and just knows what needs to be done. Everyone goes to him with questions and problems because he's been there so long he just knows how things work. His knowledge makes him responsible for more things at work it causes his co-workers to depend on him for guidance and questions.

> "But you must not eat from the tree of the knowledge of good and evil, for when you eat from it you will certainly die."
>
> *Genesis 2:17*

The bible clearly points out that knowledge equals responsibility in many different ways. Look at the original sin. Adam wasn't responsible for working the soil until he had the knowledge of good and evil. Consider Ezekiel. He was told by God to warn the people of Israel of their sins. If he failed to do what he was told then he was responsible for their deaths because they wouldn't know to correct their actions. God didn't promise Ezekiel success just that he was responsible for their failure if he didn't act. He had knowledge and was responsible for things out of his control if he didn't use it accordingly.

> "When I tell wicked people they will die because of their sins, you must warn them to turn from their sinful ways so they won't be punished. If you refuse, you are responsible for their death. However, if you do warn them, and they keep on sinning, they will die because of their sins, and you will be innocent."
>
> *Ezekiel 3:18-19*

HOW RELIGION SCREWED GOD

ALAN BETCHAN
& JOHNNY KELSEY

CONTENTS

Dedicated to Peggy Betchan, an amazing mom, grandmother, mentor, friend, leader, confidant, wife, student, and Christian. You were a mother to nearly everyone you met and you are missed more then you could have ever imagined.

I still remember it being pretty great.

If that doesn't convince you, look at what James has to say.

> If anyone, then, knows the good they ought to do and doesn't do it, it is sin for them.
>
> *James 4:17*

....

That is pretty clear; when we know something is sin we are responsible for that action. But look closer because that isn't all it's saying. It doesn't just say you are responsible for the things you do that you shouldn't, it says ALL those things that you know you should do and don't is a sin. That's right. As you understand more about what you should be doing, you have more opportunity to fail to do it, and that failure is sin. As in Ezekiel's case you may be responsible for the ignorance of others if you keep your mouth shut when GOD ASKS YOU to speak. He has made you HOLY PRIESTS.

> "And you are living stones that God is building into his spiritual temple. What's more, you are his holy priests. Through the mediation of Jesus Christ, you offer spiritual sacrifices that please God."
>
> *1 Peter 2:5*

....

Worldly people know knowledge is power, but for a Christian, knowledge is responsibility.

CONCERN AND WORRIES

Your knowledge shapes your worries. If you knew a tornado was likely to strike your home then that would consume your thoughts. All the other issues would fall to the side in light of that incredibly important information. Your knowledge of things to come determine what you worried about. This can be seen on multiple levels. You may have to worry about paying your bills for the month or what you have to get done at work tomorrow but the President of the United States has to worry about geopolitical issues on a global scale. Trade imbalances, terrorism, nuclear armament, earthquakes, global warming, race relations, and endless domestic disputes are the daily concerns of the President but how many times did you spend more than a fleeting moment contemplating any of them. The President has more knowledge than you and that knowledge determines his concerns.

If you're not yet convinced of the link between knowledge and concerns, let's consider Albert Einstein. Probably one of the single most brilliant people in modern history. His theories on physics, time, and relatively are still being sorted, debated and contemplated by scientists to this very day. Science is just now becoming technologically advanced enough to confirm the theories this man developed decades earlier.

What did a man of this level of scientific renown have to say about what was arguably his biggest applied scientific achievement?

> *"The release of atomic power has changed everything except our way of thinking ... the solution to this problem lies in the heart of mankind. If only I had known, I should have become a watchmaker."*

> **- Albert Einstein**

How about this one:

> *"I know not with what weapons World War III will be fought but World War IV will be fought with sticks and stones"*

> **- Albert Einstein**

Einstein had to worry about the effects of bringing NUCLEAR WEAPONS into the world. He had to debate the merits of contributing to research that by most accounts would not have succeeded without him. His worries and concerns were most certainly shaped by his knowledge. Lets round this out with a quote from Paul. He wrote to the church in Corinth.

> "Besides everything else, I face daily
> the pressure of my concern for all the
> churches. Who is weak, and I do not feel
> weak? Who is led into sin, and I do not
> inwardly burn?"
>
> *2 Corinthians 11:28-29*

....

When was the last time that you considered the burden your pastor endures in leading your church? When was the last time you contemplated the missionary in some backwater country that you can't even pronounce much less find on a map that daily risks his life to spread the good news of the gospel? The truth is you probably don't know any persecuted missionaries, at least personally, and you have no idea the stresses of pastoring a congregation. Your knowledge does not produce that concern. Paul on the other hand knew first hand what the early church was confronted with. He knew the persecution they faced and he had to worry about them every day. He knew they would be mocked, ridiculed, beaten, and even killed for their faith and this scripture says that it daily pressured him. His concerns were shaped by his knowledge.

PURE PAIN

How could we have a discussion about biblical knowledge and not mention Solomon. 1 Kings tells us God offered Solomon anything he desired and Solomon requested the wisdom and knowledge to lead his people. God honored this request.

> "God gave Solomon wisdom and very
> great discernment; the breadth of his
> understanding was as infinite as the sand
> on the seashore. Solomon was wiser than
> all the men of the east and all the sages
> of Egypt. He was wiser than any man,
> including Ethan the Ezrahite, or Heman,
> Calcol, and Darda, the sons of Mahol."

1 Kings 4:29-30

God made Solomon the wisest person to ever live. He gave him such wisdom that Kings come from all over the world for instruction and learning. With all that God-given wisdom and knowledge Solomon wrote:

> "For with much wisdom comes much
> sorrow: the more knowledge, the more
> grief."

Ecclesiastes 1:18

I don't believe it can be put much more plainly than that.

Wisdom=sorrow.

Knowledge=grief.

The old testament isn't the only place where we see this sentiment echoed. While Saul (who would soon change his name to Paul) was on his way to Damascus to persecute the early church Jesus Christ personally appeared to him, rebuked him for his persecution of the church, and struck him blind. He then sent him to Damascus to wait. In the meantime God sent an angel to a man named Ananias and told him to go heal Saul's blindness in Jesus' name. Ananias wasn't really excited about doing this since Saul was very publicly persecuting and frequently killing members of the early church. In response to Ananias' hesitance the Lord tells him to go because he had selected Saul to be his missionary to the Greeks. He finished off his reasoning with this.

> "And I will show him how much he must suffer for my name's sake"

> *Acts 9:16*

How much does that suck? You are called to ministry and that is your commissioning call. You are going to suffer. It is going to hurt. I'm going to bring the pain and you are going to endure it in my name. He would be arrested, run out of multiple towns, beaten on several occasions, shipwrecked, stoned, snake bitten, and ultimately martyred for his faith. For Paul the personal knowledge of Jesus was very much pain.

Not clear enough? Try Paul's words to Timothy.

> "Yes, and everyone who wants to live a godly life in Christ Jesus will suffer persecution."

> *2 Timothy 3:12*

It doesn't say may suffer.... It says, will suffer. But why?

```
    Now  if  we  are  children,  then  we
are  heirs-heirs  of  God  and  co-heirs
with  Christ,  If  indeed  we  share  in  his
sufferings  in  order  that  we  may  also
share  in  his  glory.
```

Romans 8:17

....

Perhaps the answer may be found by reviewing the Jewish nation of Israel, the people directly chosen by God. Jewish law required all Jews to adheres to 613 individual commandments.

They had to count the number of steps they took on the sabbath, offer sacrifices at set intervals, tithe, sacrifice or redeem the first fruits of their fields and first born of their livestock. They had to redeem their first born child. They had to be circumcised and follow a myriad of other laws many of which held the punishment for breaking them as death. People other than Israel were not held to these standards. They didn't have to circumcise their children or make a litany of sacrifices.

....**BUT**....

They weren't his chosen people. They didn't carry that burden but they also never got to see God work a miracle for them. He didn't part the red sea so they could cross on dry land.

He didn't lead them through the wilderness and provide for their every need. He didn't ride out before them and slay their enemies. He didn't save the world by sending his very own son through their bloodline. Israel was chosen and touched by God.   They were given knowledge of him that most certainly brought pain but also brought God's goodness and mercy.

The knowledge of God definitely brings pain, concerns, and responsibilities, but without it we cannot fulfill the purpose God has for us. We can't be his instrument of hope to a dark and dying world. We can't be the lighting rod for God's awe inspiring power. This book will hopefully bring you closer to being able to do just that.

The seriousness of the task set before you is daunting. To continue reading is an acceptance of responsibility, willingness to embrace concerns and an invitation for pain.   To put it in perspective let's review some other words written by Paul. The same man that endured all those hardships, pains and concerns wrote.

> [11]I am not saying this because I am in need, for I have learned to be content whatever the circumstances. [12]I know what it is to be in need, and I know what it is to have plenty. I have learned the secret of being content in any and every situation, whether well fed or hungry, whether living in plenty or in want. [13]I can do all this through him who gives me strength.
>
> *Philippians 4:11-13*

The same man that was commissioned to the ministry with a promise of suffering could write those words... While chained up in prison. We as Christians are not called to a life of comfort and contentment but to a life of service, sacrifice, and battle. If we show up, if we follow through, and if we commit to the cause, God will grant us the power to say what Paul wrote:

[21]For to me, to live is Christ and to die is gain. [22]If I am to go on living in the body, this will mean fruitful labor for me. Yet what shall I choose? I do not know! [23]I am torn between the two: I desire to depart and be with Christ, which is better by far; [24]but it is more necessary for you that I remain in the body.

[25]Convinced of this, I know that I will remain, and I will continue with all of you for your progress and joy in the faith, [26]so that through my being with you again your boasting in Christ Jesus will abound on account of me.

Philippians 1: 21-25

To whom much is given...much is expected.

CHAPTER 1:

SEPARATELY
IMPERFECT

THERE IS ONE GOD BUT SOMEHOW
THERE IS ALSO THREE

The power in this book comes from what could be a revelation about the Trinity. The three distinctly separate and very different existences of the same God is one of the more confusing and yet critically important Christian concepts. Mathew clearly indicates these three separate entities in Matthew chapter 3:

> "As soon as Jesus was baptized, he came up out of the water. At that moment, Heaven was opened, and he saw the Spirit of God descending like a dove and alighting on him. And a voice from heaven said, 'This is my Son, whom I love; with him I am well pleased.'"

Matthew 3:16-17

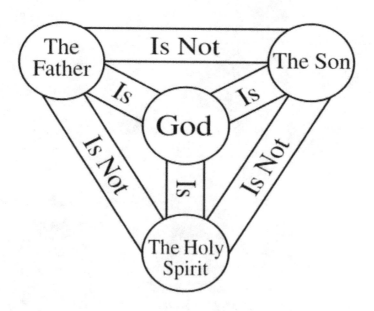

In this verse, we can clearly see three different existences in three different places: The voice of God from Heaven saying, "This is my Son, who I love," Jesus being baptized, and the Spirit of God descending like a dove – God the Father, Jesus the Son, the Holy Spirit all separately identified but somehow all still the same.

God's creation models his own divinity in so many ways. As a result there have been several great analogies that mirror the Trinity.

IN NATURE

A three-leaf clover has three separate leaves but each is still part of the same plant.

Water exists in three states – water vapor, solid ice, and liquid water – but they are all still just water. Interestingly enough, the water molecule also consists of three elements: one hydrogen to two oxygen, hence the term "H_2O."

God also created a three-dimensional universe: width, breadth and height consisting of space, time and matter.

IN MATH

A triangle has three separate sides, each necessary to create a triangle but each existing separately

IN THE OLD TESTAMENT

The Ark of the Covenant provided a way for the Israelites to experience the presence of God. Inside the Ark was—surprise, surprise—three things: the stone tablets of the Ten Commandments, mana (a miraculous food that God rained from Heaven) and the budded staff of Aaron. God can be represented in the two tablets as law and justice. The mana can be symbolized as the Holy Spirit, God's provision to his people, and Jesus can be illustrated by Aaron's staff to show Israel God's chosen priest (or maybe it was just a stick...we'll come back to this later).

Reflect: Write down an illustration of the Trinity that makes sense to you. There are several different ways the creation mirrors the creator and it's a useful exercise to unpack how you see the Trinity. Explain why it makes sense to you:

_____

_____

_____

_____

_____

_____

_____

_____

_____

_____

_____

_____

_____

_____

As useful and relevant as these are, all analogies of the Trinity are simplifications of an incomprehensible God and are therefore all inherently flawed. God is bigger, more loving and more powerful than anything we can understand. This complexity has caused many scholars and theologians to debate the relevance of the Trinity and several have dismissed the notion embracing the fact that 1) they are one being in different forms and 2) there are no significant differences in the three existences. Many, if not most, Christians know about the trinity but choose not to really unpack the idea. It's confusing and a little mystical so we'll just leave that for the pastors of the world. It doesn't really affect our understanding of God after all, right? Let's be very clear. This is wrong. The Trinity is not debatable. Jesus himself confirmed it in the Great Commission:

> "Therefore go and make disciples of all nations, baptizing them in the name of the Father and of the Son and of the Holy Spirit, and teaching them to obey everything I have commanded you. And surely I am with you always, to the very end of the age."

> *Matthew 28:19-20*

Jesus said it, so we believe it. That said, God is not an accidental God. If there are three separate instances of God then they can't be the same. If they are not the same then they must have different purposes or qualities. It is these very differences that make the trinity so critical to understanding God and our purpose on earth. Let's look at each instance.

For our purposes, we'll be using the analogy of a flame. There are three parts to a flame: smoke, heat and light. Each element exists on its own but all are actually a component of the same thing, a flame.

GOD THE FATHER...THE HEAT

"God the Father" is the form commonly referred to in the Old Testament. This makes sense when you consider that the son had not yet been born and only God's chosen prophets were granted access to the Holy Spirit. Isaiah wrote:

> "Yet you, Lord, are our Father. We are
> the clay, you are the potter; we are all
> the work of your hand."
>
> *Isaiah 64:8*

Throughout the Old Testament, God's power and his embodied presence was represented in the Ark of the Covenant. The Ark could only be approached by the Levites and even they couldn't touch it. Before it was moved, it was covered three times: with the inner curtain of the tabernacle, then with "fine goatskin," and then with a blue cloth. Finally, the Levitical priests could lift it with two long poles inserted into rings along its sides (Numbers 4:5-6). The rest of Israel would follow behind it by about 1,000 yards (Josiah 3:4); that's 10 football fields! Seems pretty crazy. Why would they need to do that? There are a couple of verses that explain why.

> 19But God struck down some of the inhabitants of Beth Shemesh, putting seventy of them to death because they looked into the ark of the Lord. The people mourned because of the heavy blow the Lord had dealt them."
>
> *1 Samuel 6:19*

> 7They set the ark of God on a new cart and brought it from the house of Abinadab, which was on the hill. Uzzah and Ahio, sons of Abinadab, were guiding the new cart with the ark of God on it, and Ahio was walking in front of it. David and all Israel were celebrating with all their might before the Lord , with castanets, harps, lyres, timbrels, sistrums and cymbals. When they came to the threshing floor of Nakon, Uzzah reached out and took hold of the ark of God, because the oxen stumbled. The Lord's

anger burned against Uzzah because of his
irreverent act; therefore God struck him
down, and he died there beside the ark
of God."

2 Samuel 6:3-7

....

God struck down a person for merely stabilizing the Ark. The Ark was quite literally the presence of the Lord on earth. When something touched by sin comes into the presence of God, it dies. He is a Holy God who cannot tolerate sin. His presence destroys it. It's not necessarily a choice, it's in his very nature. A way to conceptualize it is to think of God and his holiness as light and sin as darkness. When in presence of light darkness ceases to exist. The light didn't choose to destroy the darkness, it was just what happens when it comes in contact with it. It is the very nature of light that it can't dwell with darkness. That is the same relationship God the Father has with sin. When in his presence, sin is destroyed. In the case of a sinful person, the person is destroyed.

Let's look at the biblical characteristics of God.

He is the source of all power.

"¹⁷Ah, Sovereign Lord, you have made
the heavens and the earth by your great
power and outstretched arm. Nothing is
too hard for you."

Jeremiah 32:17

....

He is justice.

> "⁸For I, the Lord, love justice; I
> hate robbery and wrongdoing. In my
> faithfulness I will reward my people and
> make an everlasting covenant with them."
>
> *Isaiah 61:8*

··

He is vengeance and retribution.

> ³⁵It is mine to avenge; I will repay.
> In due time their foot will slip; their
> day of disaster is near and their doom
> rushes upon them."
>
> *Deuteronomy 32:35*

··

He is love.

> "⁸Whoever does not love does not know
> God, because God is love."
>
> *1 John 4:8*

··

His power is complete and he is utterly holy. It is his very words that spoke the universe into existence (though John 1 does tell us it was through the word, Jesus, that all things are made so apparently he didn't do it on his own).

> "³And God said, 'Let there be light,'
> and there was light."
>
> *Genesis 1:3*

··

Our heavenly father is the perfected dad. For most of us, our earthly father is the primary source of punishment and protection, love and discipline. It is this very dichotomy that makes God the father justice. Without retribution and punishment for wrongdoing, there can be no true justice. In our analogy he is the heat, able to grant you warmth and comfort but equally able to create pain and destruction.

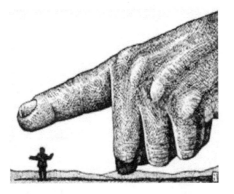

Reflect: What is your idea of God the Father? Is he the one you pray too? Is he the one you hide from? Do you see him as your loving father? Or do you see him as an angry God with Jesus saying, "Come on dad, it's alright, don't freak out and flood the earth"? Dig deep, be honest and describe the way you see God the Father in the Trinity:

_____

_____

_____

_____

_____

_____

_____

_____

_____

_____

_____

_____

_____

_____

_____

THE HOLY SPIRIT...THE SMOKE

The Holy Spirit is the conduit of God's power onto this earth. It is through the Holy Spirit that we have new life. We depend on the Spirit, because he is the only connection we have to Christ, and therefore the only way to the Father. In the Old Testament we see the Spirit of God being given to his chosen leaders and prophets. Moses even passed some of the Spirit on to other elders as we can see in the book of Numbers.

```
"Then the Lord came down in the cloud
and spoke with him, and he took some of
the power of the Spirit that was on him
and put it on the seventy elders. When the
Spirit rested on them, they prophesied -
but did not do so again."
```

Numbers 11:25

And he's always been here, as you can see in Genesis.

```
"Now the earth was formless and empty,
darkness was over the surface of the
deep, and the Spirit of God was hovering
over the waters."
```

Genesis 1:2

Yet Jesus promises to send him to us.

> "And I will ask the Father, and he will give you another advocate to help you and be with you forever – the Spirit of truth. The world cannot accept him, because it neither sees him nor knows him. But you know him, for he lives with you and will be in you."
>
> *John 14:16-17*

Let's be honest, it's a bit confusing. He's someone who's always been here and yet is being promised to come. Someone who was only with a select chosen few but now is a gift given to all who accept Christ. The Holy Spirit is something you can't see and can't hear, yet it is the way God communicates with you. It's even more confusing when John writes things like:

> "The wind blows wherever it pleases. You hear its sound, but you cannot tell where it comes from or where it is going. So it is with everyone born of the Spirit."
>
> *John 3:8*

That really clears things up doesn't it? Yet, if we review the characters of the Holy Spirit, we start to see a pattern.

He convicts us of our sin.

"And when he comes, he will convict the world of its sin, and of God's righteousness, and of the coming judgment."

John 16:8

He teaches us.

"But when the father sends the advocate as my representative – that is, the Holy Spirit – he will teach you everything and will remind you of everything I have told you."

John 14:26

He guides us into all truth.

"When the Spirit of truth comes, he will guide you into all truth. He will not speak on his own but will tell you what he has heard. He will tell you about the future. He will bring me glory by telling you whatever he receives from me. All that belongs to the Father is mine: this is why I said, The spirit will tell you whatever he receives from me."

John 16:13-15

He bears fruit through us.

"But the Holy Spirit produces this kind of fruit in our lives: love, joy, peace, patience, kindness, goodness, faithfulness, gentleness, and self control. There is no law against these things."

Galatians 5:22-23

....

He equips us with spiritual gifts.

"There are different kinds of spiritual gifts, but the same Spirit is the source of them all."

1 Cor. 12:4

....

He empowers us.

"But you will receive power when the Holy Spirit comes upon you, and you will be my witnesses, telling people about me everywhere - in Jerusalem, throughout Judea, in Samaria, and to the ends of the earth."

Acts 1:8

....

What is the common thread to each of the above characteristics? It is God enabling, communicating, or empowering us. He empowers and convicts. He teaches and equips. He guides and reminds. If God the Father is pure holy power then the Holy Spirit is the bridge that connects us to that power.

In our analogy, he is the smoke. Smoke can give you a sense that there is fire nearby but your sense of smell is imprecise. It can lead you to the fire if your senses are trained enough but it is something that can be just as easily ignored. When we don't focus on it we can become insensitive to it and not even notice it's there. This is the same with the Spirit. If we aren't seeking after the things of God we become insensitive to his callings and forget he's there.

Reflect: Think back through your life. Pick the most impactful time when it was obvious the Holy Spirit's presence was evident. It could have been a time of worship that hit you with an uncontrollable urge to lift your hands and cry or a moment when you felt severe compassion for someone for no apparent reason. Maybe it was a moment reading your Bible that did something substantial to your soul. What specific characteristic was shown in your moment? How did you feel during and/or after submitting to the Spirit? Go back and remember what he has done for you, how much he loves you, and look forward to what he will do in the future:

_____

_____

_____

_____

_____

_____

_____

_____

_____

_____

THE SON, THE LIGHT

Jesus Christ. The immaculately conceived Son of God. The final piece to the Trinity. We see stories throughout the New Testament of Jesus' amazing power and miraculous works. He healed the sick (Matthew 8:1-3), caused blind eyes to see (John 9:1-12), cast out demons (Mark 1:21-34) and raised the dead (John 11:1-44). He lived a sinless life and allowed himself to be crucified to pay the price for crimes he never committed (Galatians 3:13-15).

In our analogy he is the light – the portion of the flame that attracts the attention. It is the light that shows us where the flame is and lets us get close enough to enjoy its warmth with less risk of stumbling into the pain of being burned. Jesus himself said:

> "...I am the light of the world. Whoever follows me will never walk in darkness, but will have the light of life."
>
> *John 8:12*

....

He was wholly God.

> "The Son is the radiance of God's glory and the exact representation of his being, sustaining all things by his powerful word. After he had provided purification for sins, he sat down at the right hand of the Majesty in heaven."
>
> *Hebrews 1:3*

....

And yet he was wholly Man.

> "For this reason he had to be made like them, fully human in every way, in order that he might become a merciful and faithful high priest in service to God, and that he might make atonement for the sins of the people."
>
> *Hebrews 2:17*

How can something be wholly powerful and yet frail and fragile like a person? It's amazing that a God capable of doing all those amazing things would sacrifice his life for us. However, if he is all powerful did he really experience the same fear and temptation that we as humans experience so regularly? Would it really be that hard to live a perfect and sinless life if you were the literal incarnation of the all knowing, all seeing, all powerful God?

In the next chapter, we will discuss what it really meant for Christ to be wholly man and maybe unlock our purpose in the process.

Reflect: So what do you really think? No masks here. Don't worry about what is wrong and what is right. Simply write down what you truly believe about Christ. Don't dress it up. God knows what you really think and this is just between you and him. Do you believe he was fully man and fully God?

Do you presume he lived a perfect life because he had an unfair advantage that we don't have? Do you truly believe he was tempted just like we are tempted or do you think he had a little extra will power, divine power, to draw on? Was Jesus fully man?

_____

_____

_____

_____

_____

_____

_____

_____

_____

_____

_____

CHAPTER 2:

THE LIMITATIONS OF GOD

AN ALL POWERFUL GOD THAT DOES NOT EXCERPT FULL CONTROL

We serve a limited God.

Before you set this book aside and label it heresy, it needs to be said that God is all powerful. He is limitless (Psalm 147:5). He is capable of doing anything, anytime, anywhere. His very word created the universe as we know it (Psalm 33:6). He is the alpha and the omega. The beginning and the end (Rev. 22:13). Jeremiah wrote:

> "Ah, Sovereign Lord, you have made the heavens and the earth by your great power and outstretched arm. Nothing is too hard for you."
>
> *Jeremiah 32:17*

If that is too Old Testament for you or if you think this is just a man writing about his opinions of God, Jesus himself said:

> "... 'With man this is impossible, but with God all things are possible.'"
>
> *Matthew 19:26*

The Psalmist wrote:

> "But in my distress I cried out to the Lord; yes, I prayed to my god for help. He heard me from his sanctuary; my cry to him reached his ears. Then the earth quaked and trembled. The foundations of the mountains shook; they quaked because

of his anger. Smoke poured from his nostrils; fierce flames leaped from his mouth. Glowing coals blazed forth from him. He opened the heavens and came down; dark storm clouds were beneath his feet. Mounted on a mighty angelic being, he flew, soaring on the wings of the wind. He shrouded himself in darkness, veiling his approach with dark rain clouds. Thick clouds shielded the brightness around him and rained down hail and burning coals. The lord thundered from heaven; the voice of the most high resounded amid the hail and burning coals. He shot his arrows and scattered his enemies; great bolts of lightning flashed, and they were confused. Then at your command, O Lord, at the blast of your breath, the bottom of the sea could be seen, and the foundations of the earth were laid bare."

−Psalm 18:6−15

Did you get that picture in your mind?

Honestly at this point you should probably be questioning the validity of this book. How can a chapter titled the Limitations of God simply state that God is limitless and all powerful? It is very clear there is no disputing the omnipotence of God, but it is also very clear that he chooses to limit his power. He has created self-imposed limitations. It makes no sense to us as humans but there are some things that we have to leave to God to answer.

"For my thoughts are not your thoughts,
neither are your ways my ways," declares
the Lord . "As the heavens are higher than
the earth, so are my ways higher than your
ways and my thoughts than your thoughts."

Isaiah 55:8-9

We may not be able to understand all his motives for limiting himself but we can definitely see the effects. Perhaps looking at the ways that God chooses to limit his power will give us insight into who God really is much like it did with the trinity. In this chapter we are going to explore several specific circumstances where God has chosen to limit himself.

GOD LIMITS HIS POWER OVER HIS SPIRITUAL CREATION

This fact is probably the hardest to understand. Unfortunately for christian believers the spiritual realm is one that the Bible tends to describe in prophecy and analogy. God chose to give us glimpses of this world in various sections of scripture but our understanding of the spiritual world is very clearly limited. Angels and demons. Powers and principalities. It's all a little creepy and if we are honest, a little hard to believe. Let's start with the basics. Satan, the devil, was originally the most beautiful angel in heaven, named Lucifer. He got an idea that he could ascend the throne of God and started a war that saw him cast out of heaven. Isaiah wrote:

'How you have fallen from heaven,
morning star, son of the dawn! You have
been cast down to the earth, you who
once laid low the nations! You said
in your heart, "I will ascend to the
heavens; I will raise my throne above
the stars of God; I will sit enthroned
on the mount of assembly, on the utmost
heights of Mount Zaphon. I will ascend
above the tops of the clouds; I will
make myself like the Most High." But
you are brought down to the realm of
the dead, to the depths of the pit. '

Isaiah 14:12-15

This is further confirmed by Jesus in Luke.

'He replied, "I saw Satan fall like
lightning from heaven.'

Luke 10:18

Revelation 12:3-9 describes how this fall happened. It was a war with Michael, the angelic commander of the Lord's army, where one third of the angels in heaven choose to follow Lucifer and are cast out of heaven with him.

'Then another sign appeared in heaven:
an enormous red dragon with seven heads
and ten horns and seven crowns on its
heads. Its tail swept a third of the
stars out of the sky and flung them to the

earth. The dragon stood in front of the
woman who was about to give birth, so that
it might devour her child the moment he
was born. She gave birth to a son, a male
child, who "will rule all the nations
with an iron scepter." And her child was
snatched up to God and to his throne. The
woman fled into the wilderness to a place
prepared for her by God, where she might
be taken care of for 1,260 days. Then
war broke out in heaven. Michael and his
angels fought against the dragon, and the
dragon and his angels fought back. But
he was not strong enough, and they lost
their place in heaven. The great dragon
was hurled down—that ancient serpent
called the devil, or Satan, who leads the
whole world astray. He was hurled to the
earth, and his angels with him.'

Revelation 12:3-9

....

Think about this: You are God. You created the
heavens and the earth with nothing but your word. You
know everything and can do anything. One of your
creations, Lucifer, decides he wants to challenge you for
the throne. What do you do? Do you turn around and
speak a word that makes Satin cease to exist? Do you
challenge him to a fight where you dominate him with ease
thereby ensuring that no other portion of your creation
forgets your power? Do you utterly destroy Lucifer before
he has the chance to ruin your perfect creation, mankind,
and help them disobey?

What does Revelation say that God did? He allowed Michael and his angels to enter into a war that caused one third of his angels to be cast out of heaven. Beyond question God had the power to speak the devil out of existence. He had the power to keep his most cherished creation, humans, free from sin and dwelling with him. He had the power to end the eternal war before it ever began and yet..... he didn't. He chose to limit his power.

GOD LIMITS HIS POWER OVER OUR DECISIONS

There is no place in scripture where God forces a man to do anything. He has never imposed his will on a human. Wouldn't that have been easier than asking his prophets to do something. Surely that is within an all powerful God's power to do but we don't have a single instance of him doing so. We have numerous references to Jesus and the disciples casting demons out of people. Scripture tells us that demons had possessed people and made them mute (Matt. 12:22), made people insane and gave them superhuman strength (Mark 5:1-5), and even tried to kill the possessed person (Mark 9:22). All this evidence of fallen angels taking control of humans but, not one instance in the bible where a man is forced to do something by God.

There are several times that the holy spirit came on a person and they would worship or prophecy but these were always people that willingly chose to follow God. There isn't even a recorded instance of God inspiring a person that did not consent to it.

So the next logical question is, Why? Why would God choose to limit the implementation of his perfect will? If his will is the best possible path then why wouldn't he force it to be done? The answer to this question can give us an amazing insight into the true motivations of God. So why does he choose to allow us to make choices?

LOVE.

Think about those people in your life that you would say you truly love. Think about every time your spouse leans in close to you and whispers in your ear. Every time your mother or father tells you they are proud of you. Every time your child gives you a hug and says "I love you". Every time someone's affection for you melts your heart. Now imagine that they didn't get a choice about whether they did those things. Imagine that you MADE them love you in return.

Would that really be love. Would it really matter? Mandatory love isn't really love at all. Love can only truly exist if there is a choice to not love. If God chose, he could make every person on earth worship him right now with nothing more than a thought. But that is not what he wants. God chooses to limit himself so that we could experience true love. Love not out of duty or requirement. Love out of choice, compassion, and a desire for a relationship. Love based on trust and faith. Real love.

Reflect: Think of a time when you limited yourself for the benefit of others. Most of us are tempted to rush into a situation, take over, put the problem on our backs and save the day. After all there is nothing wrong with that since we are called to serve, protect, and defend the defenseless. But at times we are enabling or eliminating a lesson that someone needs to learn. This might be a little easier for parents. We understand our children have to learn from their mistakes and occasionally suffer the consequences of their decisions. Write down a time you have made the decision to withdraw your hand from a situation that was within your control. What was the outcome? Does it require more strength to let someone you love suffer the consequences of their own decisions? Do you think that's the same experience for God?

_____

_____

_____

_____

_____

_____

_____

_____

_____

_____

_____

JESUS LIMITED HIMSELF TO
BEING JUST A MAN

This point may be a little hard to accept at first but let's review what we know about Jesus' life prior to his baptism? Three of the four Gospels describe the amazing occurrences of Jesus' birth. We know the stories of angels' messages to Mary, Joseph, and shepherds. We know that wise men saw the coming of the foretold king and found him lying in a manger. The stories of these miraculous occurrences are detailed in the first chapters of Matthew, Mark, and Luke. Most of us know these stories from our Christmas Sunday school lessons but what happens after that? The Gospel of Luke says that Mary and Joseph went to the temple to dedicate Jesus as was required by the law. When they arrived a man named Simeon met them. This interaction is pretty amazing but is so often overlooked.

"Now there was a man in Jerusalem called Simeon, who was righteous and devout. He was waiting for the consolation of Israel, and the Holy Spirit was on him. It had been revealed to him by the Holy Spirit that he would not die before he had seen the Lord's Messiah. Moved by the Spirit, he went into the temple courts. When the parents brought in the child Jesus to do for him what the custom of the Law required, Simeon took him in his arms and praised God, saying: "Sovereign Lord, as you have promised, you may now dismiss your servant in peace. For my eyes have seen your salvation, which

you have prepared in the sight of all
nations: a light for revelation to the
Gentiles, and the glory of your people
Israel." The child's father and mother
marveled at what was said about him. Then
Simeon blessed them and said to Mary,
his mother: "This child is destined to
cause the falling and rising of many in
Israel, and to be a sign that will be
spoken against, so that the thoughts of
many hearts will be revealed. And a sword
will pierce your own soul too."

Luke 2:25-35

Pretty amazing. It seems everyone knows that this kid is something special. Sometime after the dedication of Christ the wise men presented their gifts to the baby Jesus. (Side note. The wise men did not show up on the night of Jesus' birth. Scholars believe Jesus was one year old when the wise men visited him. This aligns with the direction of Herod that all children under the age of 2 be killed. Everybody can now go home and rip the wise men out of their nativity scenes correcting this biblical fallacy.) Again, they seem to know Jesus is special. After the wise men left an angel of the lord appeared to Joseph.

'When they had gone, an angel of the
Lord appeared to Joseph in a dream. "Get
up," he said, "take the child and his
mother and escape to Egypt. Stay there
until I tell you, for Herod is going to
search for the child to kill him."

Matthew 2:13

After Herod died and it was safe to return to Judea, Mary and Joseph were warned again not to return to Nazareth.

> But when he heard that Archelaus was reigning in Judea in place of his father Herod, he was afraid to go there. Having been warned in a dream, he withdrew to the district of Galilee.
>
> *(Matthew 2:22)*

The next thing we learn about Jesus was that he failed to return home from the temple with his parents. They left assuming he was with other family members in their party and when they found out he wasn't they had to return to the temple to find him. When they found him, a day later, he was listening and asking questions of the priests. (Luke 2:41-50) After they found him the book of Luke says:

> 'Then he went down to Nazareth with them and was obedient to them. But his mother treasured all these things in her heart.'
>
> *Luke 2:51*

That's it. That's all the bible tells us about Jesus prior to his baptism. Nothing else. Really!? God became flesh, descended from heaven and dwelt among us. The all powerful creator of the universe lived with us and the only things worth recording from his first 30 years of his life were how and where he was born, his dedication at the temple, and one time when his parents misplaced him. Does this seem odd?

Let's look at this again but from a spiritual perspective. The Holy Spirit comes upon Mary causing her to immaculately conceive the son of God. He's then born with much pomp and circumstance involving angels singing and miraculous stars in the sky. Satan understands scripture and sees what's going on. He whispers to Herod that he needs to kill this child. It is apparently so real of a threat to Jesus that angels send Mary and Joseph into hiding. Then nothing....not a word. No spiritual battles where the Lord's angels defend the infant son of God. No miraculous defense of himself where Jesus tells demons to be gone. Nothing. All we get is:

> `'And    Jesus    grew    in    wisdom    and`
> `stature, and in favor with God and man.'`

> *Luke 2:52*

....

The people of his hometown after he had started his ministry even said.

> `        They  asked,  "Where  did  he  get  all`
> `this  wisdom  and  the  power  to  perform`
> `such miracles?" Then they scoffed, "He's`
> `just  a  carpenter,  the  son  of  Mary  and`
> `the  brother  of  James,  Joseph,  Judas,  and`
> `Simon.  And  his  sisters  live  right  here`
> `among  us."  They  were  deeply  offended  and`
> `refused to believe in him.`

> *Mark 6:2-3*

....

Jesus was so normal that the people who he grew up among could not believe the miracles in spite of the fact they had seen them and heard his teaching in person. He was so ordinary growing up that "They were deeply offended and refused to believe in him."

Let's be honest, if an angel sent you into hiding so that the ruler of your country couldn't kill your miraculously born son, would you be discussing his divinity with anyone? Every parent wants to protect their children but aren't you going to be a little extra careful with the son of God? If he had performed miracles as he was growing up wouldn't someone have noticed? If there had been something special or powerful about him wouldn't that make it easy for those that grew up with him to accept his miracles?

Though compelling, these facts may be dismissed as circumstantial and are certainly not definitive. Let's examine a more explicit example of the humanity of Christ.

All of the gospels mention John the Baptist. What we know about him was his mother Elizabeth was a "relative" of Mary the mother of God. Luke chapter 1 goes into great detail about the miraculous foretelling of the birth of John and the explanation of Gabriel to his father that John would "make ready a people prepared for the Lord"(Luke 1:17). Basically, John was empowered by the Holy Spirit, before his birth, to go and start preparing the people of Israel for the coming of Christ. After Mary is told she will give birth to Christ she visits Elizabeth.

'When Elizabeth heard Mary's greeting,
the baby leaped in her womb, and Elizabeth
was filled with the Holy Spirit. In a loud
voice she exclaimed: "Blessed are you
among women, and blessed is the child you
will bear! But why am I so favored, that
the mother of my Lord should come to me?
As soon as the sound of your greeting
reached my ears, the baby in my womb
leaped for joy. Blessed is she who has
believed that the Lord would fulfill his
promises to her!"

Luke 1:41-45

....

Basically, Elizabeth knows Mary is carrying the Son of
God. Mary even lives with her for several months. Fast
forward thirty years and John is the person who baptizes
Jesus. John Chapter 1 has a very interesting testimony
about Jesus from John himself.

'The next day John saw Jesus coming
toward him and said, "Look, the Lamb of
God, who takes away the sin of the world!
This is the one I meant when I said,
'A man who comes after me has surpassed
me because he was before me.' I myself
did not know him, but the reason I came
baptizing with water was that he might
be revealed to Israel." Then John gave
this testimony: "I saw the Spirit come
down from heaven as a dove and remain on
him. And I myself did not know him, but
the one who sent me to baptize with water

told me, 'The man on whom you see the
Spirit come down and remain is the one
who will baptize with the Holy Spirit.'
I have seen and I testify that this is
God's Chosen One."

John 1:29-34

....

Take that in. John, the cousin of Jesus, the person sent
to prepare the people of Israel for his coming didn't know
that Jesus was the Messiah! If Jesus had been doing
miraculous things then wouldn't he have known he was
the Son of God? If the family had discussed the divinity of
Jesus wouldn't he have heard?

The enemy tried so hard to kill Jesus after his
miraculous birth. Satan was so thorough that he had
Herod kill all male kids born within a year of Jesus. The
devil knows scripture and understood the prophecy of
Emmanuel but after he was born you never hear about the
devil trying to get rid of the savior as a toddler, or a boy, or
a teenager, or a young man.

Why? Because Christ chose to limit himself to the
existence of a normal ordinary man. He was truly no
different then you and I with the exception that he did
not inherit a nature of sin. How could Satan not destroy
a simple boy before the beginning of his ministry? He
couldn't find him. He never drew on any kind of divine
power to reveal himself as being any different than
any other person. He was just a guy like every other

man. Nothing special or miraculous. He had to endure everything that you and I endure without any special power to help him along the path.

To understand the importance of Christ being fully man there is one thing that needs to be perfectly clear in your mind. God gave dominion over the Earth to man.

> Then God blessed them and said, "Be fruitful and multiply. Fill the earth and govern it. Reign over the fish in the sea, the birds in the sky, and all the animals that scurry along the ground."
>
> *Genesis 1:28 NLT*

And man gave that dominion to Satan.

> Satan, who is the god of this world, has blinded the minds of those who don't believe. They are unable to see the glorious light of the Good News. They don't understand this message about the glory of Christ, who is the exact likeness of God.
>
> *2 Corinthians 4:4 NLT*

And by giving dominion to Satan they allowed death into the world.

> "It's only the fruit from the tree in the middle of the garden that we are not allowed to eat. God said, 'You must not eat it or even touch it; if you do, you will die."
>
> *Genesis 3:3 NLT*

....

> By the sweat of your brow will you have food to eat until you return to the ground from which you were made. For you were made from dust, and to dust you will return."
>
> *Genesis 3:19 NLT*

....

So since God gave dominion to man. The word had to be saved by a man and death had to be defeated by a man.

> So you see, just as death came into the world through a man, now the resurrection from the dead has begun through another man. Just as everyone dies because we all belong to Adam, everyone who belongs to Christ will be given new life.
>
> *1 Corinthians 15:21-22 NLT*

....

Jesus was not capable of doing the very thing he was sent to do unless he did so as a. An ordinary, tempted, frail, and simple man.

Reflect: Does the realization that Jesus was a normal human change your perspective of temptation? What do you think of the fact that he faced the same temptations that you face? The same desires. The fact that he was just like you. That he had no special power or divine advantage yet he lived a perfect life. How does this make you view your temptations? What about the fact Jesus resisted the same temptations for 30 years alone and on his own strength? Does it make you feel ashamed and weak?

Don't.

Celebrate the fact that we don't have to do the same thing thanks to his sacrifice. Now we fight those temptations with the help of the Holy Spirit. Not alone but side by side. Now's the time to take control. Make a decision to define your biggest temptation and take it to God. Shed your excuses, shed your justifications, realize who you are and realize exactly what you have. You are a child of God empowered by his living spirit. The same spirit that raised Christ from the dead dwells in you! Temptation has no power here. Give that hidden temptation a name and confess it to a fellow christian you trust. Find healing for that pain right now, not by your own strength, but by the power invested in you by God.

_____

_____

_____

_____

_____

_____

_____

_____

_____

_____

_____

_____

_____

_____

_____

_____

God limits his power's ability to be manifested on the earth. God chooses to work through man... every time.

The next chapter will dig deeper into this limitation and explore the impact of Christ on it.

CHAPTER 3:

THE PERFECT
STICK

ALL GOD NEEDS IS A STICK

JESUS GAVE US THE PERFECT EXAMPLE OF HOW TO LIVE IN THE SPIRIT'S POWER

Pastor Jentezen Franklin once taught a message titled Just a stick. The gist of the message was that God doesn't need something to be miraculous in order for him to work a miracle. In fact it's just the opposite, he wants the ordinary. The simple. Just a stick. He used the example of Moses and his staff. That same stick turned into a serpent, parted the red sea, made water come from a rock, and led Israel to victory in battle. Pastor Franklin's point was that it was just a stick. Nothing special or amazing but it had everything that God needed to produce his will.

Before we dig deeper into the concept of The Perfect Stick let's go back and develop the last point from Chapter 2.

GOD LIMITS HIS ABILITY TO MANIFEST HIS POWER ON THE EARTH

One consistent theme that echoes throughout the new and the old testament is God's choice to act through a person. When God wanted to lead Israel out of captivity he sent Moses to speak to the pharaoh and call down the 10 plagues. God could have spoken to pharaoh in a dream if he chose. In fact he did speak to pharaoh in a dream in Genesis chapter 41 (This is where God sends two dreams to pharaoh that could not be interpreted by anyone except Joseph). Instead of doing that again, he sends Moses to challenge the pharaohs mystics and lead the Israelites out of Egypt. When they came to the Red Sea God could have split the water as soon as they approached or even when the pillar of fire drew near to the sea. Instead Exodus tells us...

> "Then the Lord said to Moses, "Why are you crying out to me? Tell the Israelites to move on. Raise your staff and stretch out your hand over the sea to divide the water so that the Israelites can go through the sea on dry ground."

Exodus 14:15-16

When the Israelites were entering the promised land the first place they came to was the great walled city of Jericho. God gave Joshua special instructions on how to defeat the city.

> "Then the Lord said to Joshua, "See, I have delivered Jericho into your hands, along with its king and its fighting men. March around the city once with all the armed men. Do this for six days. Have seven priests carry trumpets of rams' horns in front of the ark. On the seventh day, march around the city seven times, with the priests blowing the trumpets. When you hear them sound a long blast on the trumpets, have the whole army give a loud shout; then the wall of the city will collapse and the army will go up, everyone straight in."

Joshua 6:2-5

At first glance this doesn't seem that unusual (other than the fact the lord is destroying a wall with mere noise). God needed Joshua to march around the city so they could be given victory. But this is the same God that sent fire and brimstone to destroy Sodom and Gomorrah. Couldn't he have done that again? It's even more odd when you read what happened right before the Lord told Joshua to march around the city.

> "Now when Joshua was near Jericho, he looked up and saw a man standing in front of him with a drawn sword in his hand. Joshua went up to him and asked, "Are you for us or for our enemies?" "Neither," he replied, "but as commander of the army of the Lord I have now come." Then Joshua fell facedown to the ground in reverence, and asked him, "What message does my Lord have for his servant?" The commander of the Lord's army replied, "Take off your sandals, for the place where you are standing is holy." And Joshua did so."

Joshua 5:13-15

The commander of the Lord's army, the archangel Michael, was already at Jericho when Joshua arrived. God could have easily used Michael to destroy Jericho but instead he chose to have Joshua march around the city.

The natural argument against God consistently using a man is his divine retribution. Divine retribution is a very church term but it basically means his justified wrath being poured out on someone. It is a justified godly consequence for sin. Good examples of this are the flood of Noah, the destruction of Sodom and Gomorrah, the plagues breaking out among the Israelites while they were in the wilderness, and the exile of the Israelites. These are times when God supernaturally caused disaster to befall people. Each of those times he does it without a person requesting that action (at least no one is recorded as requesting them in the Bible).

Oddly though everytime you see the divine retribution of God you also see God discussing it with a man first or a man already being in place to immediately intercede for the people thereafter. This is seen in numerous places in the old testament. Abraham interceded for Abimelech when he took his wife (Genesis 20:17). Moses interceded when the people of Israel created the golden cafe (Deu. 9:18). In the book of Amos, Amos asked God not to release punishment on Israel several times before they were sent into exile. Even after Israel was exiled Ezekiel prayed for God's anger to relent:

> "Now as I was prophesying, Pelatiah son of Benaiah died. Then I fell face down and cried out in a loud voice, "Alas, Sovereign Lord ! Will you completely destroy the remnant of Israel?" '
>
> *Ezekiel 11:13*

The book of Malachi tells us:

"I the Lord do not change. So you, the descendants of Jacob, are not destroyed."

Malachi 3:6

This seems inconsistent since he changed his actions several times at the request of a man. If the Lord does not change then he must have WANTED someone to ask for his anger to be stayed. He must have been looking for someone to intercede. The entire story of Jonah shows this. He was literally sending Jonah to Nineveh to ask them to change their ways. This can be seen again in the new testament when Peter writes.

"The Lord is not slow in keeping his promise, as some understand slowness. Instead he is patient with you, not wanting anyone to perish, but everyone to come to repentance."

2 Peter 3:9

God doesn't change so the same God that flooded the earth also didn't want anyone to perish. God wanted a reason to stay his wrath. God wanted someone to intercede.

God's wrath is one of the more confusing aspects of the Bible. The same God who sacrificed his son to forgive our sins also destroyed the world in a flood. At first glance it appears God might be a little bipolar or at the least mildly schizophrenic. A God whose grace is unending is also the God who punishes the wicked. The simple truth is God's very nature demands justice which is necessarily wrathful when sin is involved. That same nature, love, also desires grace which can be brought about by the simple request of a righteous man. The question becomes why don't we see God's wrath more frequently today. In a world gone astray there is probably as much, if not more, sin deserving of judgment than existed in Sodom. So why don't we see him raining fire on those sinful institutions? The bible holds the answer to this question as well.

> "Who then is the one who condemns? No one. Christ Jesus who died—more than that, who was raised to life—is at the right hand of God and is also interceding for us."
>
> *Romans 8:34*

The difference now is that Christ has paid the price for sin so we no longer have to experience God's wrath. Simply put God sent the perfect intercessor!

THE PERFECT STICK

Since we've established that Jesus was perfectly human the natural question is 'How did he perform miracles?' The quick answer is he was the son of God. That gives him a little extra juice, right? When you are immaculately conceived by the Spirit of God you should have some miraculous abilities. But this doesn't align with what we've established about Jesus' humanity.

If he was just a man how did he do so many great miracles that he was distinguished from every prophet and judge that came before him? Why did so many people believe he was the savior and the foretold king even before the resurrection? The answer to this confusion can be found in the title of this Chapter.

JESUS WAS THE PERFECT STICK

Let's review what we've established and apply it to this truth. God is a Triune God existing in the three distinct entities with three distinct purposes. The father is the source of the power and the Holy Spirit is the conduit for his power into our reality. God chooses to limit how he interacts with our world and Jesus was simply a man for the first thirty years of his life. If we apply those truths to this statement we can say Jesus was just a man until the Holy Spirit descended on him at baptism and provided the conduit for God's power to be used by him. Let's look again at what happened at the time of Jesus' baptism.

> "At that time Jesus came from Nazareth in Galilee and was baptized by John in the Jordan. Just as Jesus was coming up out of the water, he saw heaven being torn open and the Spirit descending on him like a dove. And a voice came from heaven: "You are my Son, whom I love; with you I am well pleased."
>
> *Mark 1:9-11*

Interestingly this is one of the few stories of Jesus' life that is found in all four Gospels. Each Gospel recognizes this as the beginning of his ministry and each describes the spirit descending and God speaking. It must be pretty important for it to be in all four Gospels. Equally interesting is what happens immediately after the baptism.

"At once the Spirit sent him out into the wilderness, and he was in the wilderness forty days, being tempted by Satan. He was with the wild animals, and angels attended him."

Mark 1:12-13

Suddenly, when Jesus is connected to the Father by the Spirit, Satan takes notice. He is immediately sent by the spirit into the wilderness where he is tempted by Satan. Thirty years of no written interaction between Satan and Jesus then he's baptized and Satan comes to the party. Why? Because Jesus pops up on the spiritual 'radar' when he's baptized because he's now connected to the conduit of the Father's power... the Holy Spirit.

Keep in mind, there are no recorded miracles performed by Jesus prior to his baptism. Not one. Combine this information with the knowledge we have about the sudden and immediate spiritual temptation of Jesus we can assume that the descent of the spirit onto Jesus is what enabled him to perform miracles. Jesus appears to confirm this in John.

"Jesus gave them this answer: "Very
truly I tell you, the Son can do nothing
by himself; he can do only what he sees
his Father doing, because whatever the
Father does the Son also does."

John 5:19

....

He further attests.

"By myself I can do nothing; I judge
only as I hear, and my judgment is just,
for I seek not to please myself but him
who sent me."

John 5:30

....

But if that is the case then why wasn't every old
testament prophet performing miracles like Jesus did?
The answer can be found in his divine nature. The only
difference between Jesus and every other person was he
didn't inherit a sin nature. Every person born of a man,
inherits the sin nature of the decision Adam and Eve made.

By eating of the Tree of Knowledge we inherit that
knowledge and the cost of that knowledge which is death.

'Therefore, just as sin entered the
world through one man, and death through
sin, and in this way death came to all
people, because all sinned—"

Romans 5:12

....

Jesus is different. He was conceived by the Holy Spirit and therefore did not inherit this sin nature. This allowed him to dwell **PERFECTLY** with the Holy Spirit. A perfect and seamless interaction between man (the thing that God chooses to use to implement his will and power on earth) and the Holy Spirit (the conduit for God's power and the entity that communicates the Father's will). This enabled Christ to perform the amazing miracles that set him apart from every spirit led prophet before him. A perfect stick.

So why are we here? That is a big question right. What is the meaning of life, the universe and everything? Many people struggle with this and those that don't just ignore it. Lean into this one, let it penetrate your soul and conflict your mind. Stretch your understanding and let this sink in through prayer and meditation. Pray that the Spirit reveals your role in this war, and write your answer below.

_____

_____

_____

_____

_____

The application of the fact Jesus was just the perfect stick should be something that changes the way you live your life every day. We've established that Jesus was human and able to perform the miracles he performed because of his sinless nature that allowed him to dwell perfectly with the Spirit. We, however, do not have a sinless nature so we don't have the ability to dwell with the spirit as Jesus did, right? If that's the case then why did Jesus say.

> "Very truly I tell you, whoever believes in me will do the works I have been doing, and they will do even greater things than these, because I am going to the Father."
>
> *John 14:12*

This doesn't seem to make sense. How can we do greater things than Jesus if we have a sin nature? Let's consider Jesus' crucifixion. The crucifixion really begins the night of the passover feast in the upper room. Jesus reveals that Judas will be the disciple that betrays him and the bible tells us something very unusual.

> 'Then Satan entered Judas, called Iscariot, one of the Twelve. And Judas went to the chief priests and the officers of the temple guard and discussed with them how he might betray Jesus."
>
> *Luke 22:3-4*

Not once but twice.

> "When Judas had eaten the bread, Satan entered into him. Then Jesus told him, "Hurry and do what you're going to do."

John 13:27 NLT

....

That's a very unique statement. Nowhere else in the bible does it say Satan himself possesses a man. And to do it at such a pivotal moment in history means it was intentionally done. Satan himself chose to make sure Christ would be crucified. Satan isn't ignorant of scripture, in fact, he actually tempted Jesus using scripture when he was in the wilderness

> 'Then the devil took him to the holy city and had him stand on the highest point of the temple. "If you are the Son of God," he said, "throw yourself down. For it is written: "He will command his angels concerning you, and they will lift you up in their hands, so that you will not strike your foot against a stone."

Matthew 4:5-6

....

Satan knew that old testament prophets foretold his coming.

> "But you, Bethlehem Ephrathah, though you are small among the clans of Judah, out of you will come for me one who will be ruler over Israel, whose origins are from of old, from ancient times."
>
> *Micah 5:2*

So Satan knew Jesus was here to save mankind so why would he help in that effort? Perhaps Satan thought that killing Jesus was the ultimate victory. Jesus had spent his ministry enabling his followers to cast out demons and preach repentance. Removing Jesus would allow things to return to what they had historically been. Simply put, killing Jesus would send him back to heaven and let Satan continue ruling the world. What changed that? What made it a win for God and not a win for Satan?

> "He himself bore our sins" in his body on the cross, so that we might die to sins and live for righteousness; "by his wounds you have been healed."
>
> *1 Peter 2:24*

The moment that Jesus became sin on the cross he lost his perfect connection with the Father.

> "About three in the afternoon Jesus
> cried out in a loud voice, "Eli, Eli,
> lema sabachthani?" (which me and "My God,
> my God, why have you forsaken me?").""
>
> *Matthew 27:46*

....

Jesus could no longer dwell perfectly with the Holy Spirit and it hurt him. He was alone and hurting and unable to dwell with his father. He was wholly man.

Perhaps this is the time that Satan realized he made a mistake. He thought he was sending Jesus back to heaven but now, since he took on our sins, he was no longer bound for heaven. He was bound for death.

> "What does "he ascended" mean except
> that he also descended to the lower,
> earthly regions?"
>
> *Ephesians 4:9*

....

In other words, he was heading to Satan's domain. There he waged war and conquered death. This was apparently for those who had already died as well. Matthew says.

> "At that moment the curtain of the
> temple was torn in two from top to bottom.
> The earth shook, the rocks split and the
> tombs broke open. The bodies of many holy
> people who had died were raised to life.
> They came out of the tombs after Jesus'
> resurrection and went into the holy city
> and appeared to many people.
>
> *Matthew 27:51-53*

....

That is pretty amazing. The spiritual world is turned upside down. Old saints, long since dead, are released from death and resurrected with Jesus. This represented a massive change in the world but what does it mean for you and I personally? Is it just that we get to miss hell and get into heaven? Let's look at what Hebrews has to say.

> 'Day after day every priest stands and performs his religious duties; again and again he offers the same sacrifices, which can never take away sins. But when this priest had offered for all time one sacrifice for sins, he sat down at the right hand of God, and since that time he waits for his enemies to be made his footstool. For by one sacrifice he has made perfect forever those who are being made holy.'

> *Hebrews 10:11-14*

His sacrifice made us Holy. When we accept Jesus as our lord and Saviour all of our sins are paid for. We are blameless. Suddenly we are perfect and can dwell perfectly with the Holy Spirit. The devil thought he was killing the one perfect stick but really by doing so he made millions more.

JESUS DIDN'T COME JUST TO SET YOU FREE, HE CAME TO TURN YOU LOOSE.

He didn't just come and unlock your chains and say go free. He came and unlocked your chains then handed you a gun and said let's get em.

Let that sink in.

He didn't just die to get you into heaven. He died to make you the perfect warrior. He came to connect you perfectly to the power of God. If you really believe that it should change your perception of why we are here. How do we find out what God wants and tell him what we want? Prayer.

The act of talking with God. Prayer has the power to do anything God can do and we are called to pray. If the church really believed this the world would be changed quickly. We'd see the miracles of the early church regularly. We'd see people being healed by their pastors shadow (Acts 5:15), we'd see earthquakes following our prayers (Acts 4:31), we'd see great wonders and signs (Acts 6:8), we'd see all needs of the church being met(Acts 4:34) and we'd see Satan running in fear.

Unfortunately, the devil is very good at what he does. to make you ineffective in the war he doesn't really need to send you in the completely wrong direction. He convinces us these miracles are for the early church apostles and not us. He convinces us it's about how much we give or how often we serve. He has convinced the church we are here to get souls into heaven when the reality is we are here to pray heaven down to earth.

What if God has a list of things he would like to do, things that he wills to happen, that never come to fruition because YOU failed to pray them into existence? What if there are diseases he'd like to heal, marriages he'd like to restore, hearts he would like to mend, and nations he'd like to save all of which never get done because we didn't ask God to intercede. What if the current ungodly state of the world is simply because his church isn't effectively engaged in the one thing that will change it...Prayer.

That's it. That's the whole point of this book. If you don't believe the above you might as well quit reading. BUT BEFORE YOU DO go back and read the forward. Remember, we will be held accountable for not doing the things we ought to.

God uses sticks. Jesus' power was found in the Holy Spirit which he sent to us. Realize your role. Don't lean on your own understanding, realize that with man it's impossible but with God all things are possible. You are not God and God only uses sticks because the stick knows it's nothing unless it is in the hand of the Shepherd. Now it's time to start asking God for more snake moments.

CHAPTER 4:

HOW BIG IS YOUR HOSE?

FAITH - THE CONDUIT OF GOD'S POWER

IT IS ONLY YOUR FAITH THAT LIMITS GOD'S POWER

Faith is one of the most churchy of words. Most of us have an idea of what it is (or what we think it is) but we generally don't have true respect and reverence for how important our faith really is. Faith determines the amount of God's power he is able to exert on earth. To truly understand God let's look at one final pivotal point regarding God's self imposed limitations.

GOD HAS NEVER DONE ANYTHING ON EARTH UNLESS IT WAS DONE THROUGH THE FAITH OF A MAN

Think back on the biblical stories you can. Every pivotal moment in the history of God, after man's creation, was based on the faith of a man. God became a man and was born into this world but Abraham had to offer Isaac as a sacrifice to demonstrate his faith.(Genesis 22:1-19) God delivered Abraham's people from the Egyptians by way of plagues but Moses had to walk into Pharaoh and demand that he let his people go. Moses spoke the word of the plague and it was so. God parted the red sea but Moses had to raise his staff. God had Israel win their battle against the Amalekites but again Moses had to hold his hands up to win.(Exodus 17:11-13). God demolished the walls of Jericho but the Israelites had to have the faith to march around seven times first.(Joshua 6:20). God made the sun stand still but Joshua had to have the faith to ask God for it.(Joshua 10:12)

The old testament necessity for faith can be presented no better than it was in Hebrews chapter 11.

Reflection: Take some time and really read Hebrews 11 below to yourself. Before you begin pray that the spirit speaks to you through the text. We are trying to get our hearts in the right place before continuing with this chapter. Once you have finished the chapter right down the points that really stick out, speak to, or challenge you. Try and dig deep

¹Now faith is confidence in what we hope for and assurance about what we do not see. ²This is what the ancients were commended for.

³By faith we understand that the universe was formed at God's command, so that what is seen was not made out of what was visible.

⁴By faith Abel brought God a better offering than Cain did. By faith he was commended as righteous, when God spoke well of his offerings. And by faith Abel still speaks, even though he is dead.

⁵By faith Enoch was taken from this life, so that he did not experience death: "He could not be found, because God had taken him away." For before he was taken, he was commended as one who pleased God.

⁶And without faith it is impossible to please God, because anyone who comes to him must believe that he exists and that he rewards those who earnestly seek him.

⁷By faith Noah, when warned about things not yet seen, in holy fear built an ark to save his family. By his faith he condemned the world and became heir of the righteousness that is in keeping with faith.

⁸By faith Abraham, when called to go to a place he would later receive as his inheritance, obeyed and went, even though he did not know where he was going. ⁹By faith he made his home in the promised land like a stranger in a foreign country; he lived in tents, as did Isaac and Jacob, who were heirs with him of the same promise. 10For he was looking forward to the city with foundations, whose architect and builder is God. ¹¹And by faith even Sarah, who was past childbearing age, was enabled to bear children because she considered him faithful who had made the promise. ¹²And so from this one man, and he as good as dead, came descendants as numerous as the stars in the sky and as countless as the sand on the seashore.

¹³All these people were still living by faith when they died. They did not receive the things promised; they only saw them and welcomed them from a distance, admitting that they were foreigners and strangers on earth. ¹⁴People who say such things show that they are looking for a country of their own. ¹⁵If they had been thinking of the country they had left, they would have had opportunity to return.

¹⁶Instead, they were longing for a better country—a heavenly one. Therefore God is not ashamed to be called their God, for he has prepared a city for them.

¹⁷By faith Abraham, when God tested him, offered Isaac as a sacrifice. He who had embraced the promises was about to sacrifice his one and only son, ¹⁸even though God had said to him, "It is through Isaac that your offspring will be reckoned." ¹⁹Abraham reasoned that God could even raise the dead, and so in a manner of speaking he did receive Isaac back from death.

²⁰By faith Isaac blessed Jacob and Esau in regard to their future.

²¹By faith Jacob, when he was dying, blessed each of Joseph's sons, and worshiped as he leaned on the top of his staff.

²²By faith Joseph, when his end was near, spoke about the exodus of the Israelites from Egypt and gave instructions concerning the burial of his bones.

²³By faith Moses' parents hid him for three months after he was born, because they saw he was no ordinary child, and they were not afraid of the king's edict.

²⁴By faith Moses, when he had grown up, refused to be known as the son of Pharaoh's daughter.

²⁵He chose to be mistreated along with the people of God rather than to enjoy the fleeting pleasures of sin. ²⁶He regarded disgrace for the sake of Christ as of greater value than the treasures of Egypt, because he was looking ahead to his reward. ²⁷By faith he left Egypt, not fearing the king's anger; he persevered because he saw him who is invisible. ²⁸By faith he kept the Passover and the application of blood, so that the destroyer of the firstborn would not touch the firstborn of Israel.

²⁹By faith the people passed through the Red Sea as on dry land; but when the Egyptians tried to do so, they were drowned.

³⁰By faith the walls of Jericho fell, after the army had marched around them for seven days.

³¹By faith the prostitute Rahab, because she welcomed the spies, was not killed with those who were disobedient.

³²And what more shall I say? I do not have time to tell about Gideon, Barak, Samson and Jephthah, about David and Samuel and the prophets, ³³who through faith conquered kingdoms, administered justice, and gained what was promised; who shut the mouths of lions, ³⁴quenched the fury of the flames, and escaped the edge of the sword; whose weakness was turned to strength; and who became powerful in battle and routed foreign armies. ³⁵Women received back their

dead, raised to life again. There were others who were tortured, refusing to be released so that they might gain an even better resurrection. [36]Some faced jeers and flogging, and even chains and imprisonment. [37]They were put to death by stoning; they were sawed in two; they were killed by the sword. They went about in sheepskins and goatskins, destitute, persecuted and mistreated— [38]the world was not worthy of them. They wandered in deserts and mountains, living in caves and in holes in the ground.

[39]These were all commended for their faith, yet none of them received what had been promised, [40]since God had planned something better for us so that only together with us would they be made perfect.

Hebrews 11:1-39

_____

_____

_____

_____

_____

_____

_____

_____

At this point we can see the thread of faith weaved throughout the old testament and the disciples and the early church certainly demonstrate the importance of faith. It can be said no more clearly than Paul's writings to the church in Ephesus.

> "⁸For it is by grace you have been saved, through faith—and this is not from yourselves, it is the gift of God—
>
> *Ephesians 2:8*

But what does Jesus have to say about faith? One of the most telling scriptures about the relationship between Jesus and faith can be seen in the Gospel of Matthew. Jesus had been traveling the region near Galilee teaching the people with his disciples and performing healings. He came to his hometown and the people were amazed. They questioned where he got this wisdom and how he did these miraculous things. They said, Isn't this Mary and Joseph's son? We know where he grew up. We know he is just an ordinary guy. Then scripture tells us a very enlightening statement.

> "⁵⁸And he did not do many miracles there because of their lack of faith."
>
> *Mathew 13:58*

Wow! The power of Jesus, the son of God, was limited by the lack of faith of those around him. That makes it pretty important. Jesus Christ himself was limited by the faith of those people around him. He wasn't only limited by other faiths he was also enabled by it. The most telling scripture of this is the story of his first miracle.

[1]On the third day a wedding took place at Cana in Galilee. Jesus' mother was there, [2]and Jesus and his disciples had also been invited to the wedding. [3]When the wine was gone, Jesus' mother said to him, "They have no more wine." [4]"Woman, why do you involve me?" Jesus replied. "My hour has not yet come." [5]His mother said to the servants, "Do whatever he tells you." [6]Nearby stood six stone water jars, the kind used by the Jews for ceremonial washing, each holding from twenty to thirty gallons. [7]Jesus said to the servants, "Fill the jars with water"; so they filled them to the brim.

[8]Then he told them, "Now draw some out and take it to the master of the banquet." They did so, [9]and the master of the banquet tasted the water that had been turned into wine. He did not realize where it had come from, though the servants who had drawn the water knew. Then he called the bridegroom aside [10]and said, "Everyone brings out the choice wine first and then the cheaper wine after the guests have had too much to drink; but you have saved the best till now."

> [11]What Jesus did here in Cana of Galilee
> was the first of the signs through which
> he revealed his glory; and his disciples
> believed in him."

John 2:1-11

....

At first glance this scripture seems to show Jesus as fickle or prone to changing his mind. Jesus clearly tells Mary it's not yet his time then he turns around and performs his first miracle. If it's not his time then why did he perform the miracle? The answer? Mary's faith. Let's look at her response to Jesus' denial of her request.

> "[5]His mother said to the servants, "Do
> whatever he tells you."

John 2:5

....

Mary's response to Jesus' denial was to ignore his response and instruct the servants to do what he says. She had faith that he would perform a miracle. Her faith brought about Jesus' time and ultimately began his ministry.

DID JESUS HAVE FAITH?

Since we have established the necessity and importance of faith we should try to understand what it is. The best way to do that is by asking the question, "Did Jesus have Faith"? Let's look at the facts. If faith is necessary for miracles and Jesus was unable to do miracles without the faith of those around him then he must not have had faith of his own. This certainly appears to agree with the story of him in Nazareth. It's interesting that this is a point of theological debate that goes back hundreds of years. Thomas Aquinas was a Catholic priest that lived in the 13th century whom was ultimately sainted by the church. He believed that faith required a person to be lacking something, i.e. knowledge, and therefore since Christ was perfect and lacked nothing he could not have had faith. That agrees with the concept of faith strictly presented in Hebrews 11:1:

> "Now faith is confidence in what we hope for and assurance about what we do not see."
>
> *Hebrews 11:1*

How would Jesus have faith in something that he knew existed. He can't have assurance of something unseen if he knows it to be there, i.e. he has physically been in the presence of God. At first glance this appears to be the end of the debate. Jesus didn't have faith. Turn the page and read Hebrews 12:1-2:

> "[1]Therefore, since we are surrounded by such a great cloud of witnesses, let us throw off everything that hinders and the sin that so easily entangles. And let us run with perseverance the race marked out for us, [2]fixing our eyes on Jesus, the pioneer and perfecter of faith."
>
> *Hebrews 12:1-2*

Jesus is the pioneer of our faith? How is that possible if he doesn't himself possess it. Other versions use the terms the author or champion and initiator. All of these indicate he is the inception of faith.

If both answers seem to be supported (and assuming the Bible is the infallible word of God) it must mean that we don't understand the question. But the question is simple: Did Jesus have faith? Only four words and three of them are fairly indisputable. The only thing that we might not have a full grasp of is faith. Perhaps we have a definition issue. So now we arrive at the crux of the question. What is faith?

Reflection: Now it is time to really see what you believe faith is. This is the single most important aspect to the development of a christian and the odds are you think you have a clear definition in your mind but dig deeper. Take the time you need. What is the definition of faith for you. This should not be the Merriem Webster definition, not a church answer, and not something you just heard before. Is it a noun or a verb? What does it really mean to you? Pray then write down what you think.

_____

_____

_____

_____

_____

_____

_____

_____

_____

_____

_____

_____

Not as easy as it sounded is it? Were you able to come up with an answer? Are you a little shocked that it was as difficult as it was? Odd that something so integral to our faith, pun intended, is so undefined. This isn't just you. If you do a quick google search for a definition of the word faith you will find that it varies wildly. Why is there a lack of consensus on something so core to our relationship with God? The answer: Christians understanding the definition of faith is important to Satan too. If faith is the key to bringing God's power to bear on the earth through prayer, then keeping its purpose clouded is critical to the success of the enemy. He needs there to be confusion and questioning to keep you from the power of God. He doesn't want you engaged in the war. If our enemy is trying to cloak it in confusion then there must be power in the answer. Let's test this definition.

Faith-A trust in the word and goodness of God that is deep enough to create willingness to act.

Faith is a belief in action. It is knowing something with such certainty that you are willing to rely on it. A great example is a chair. Take a look at the chair you are sitting in. You review the chair, you consider the material it is constructed of, the structure of the chair, and the quality of the construction. You believe the chair will hold you when you sit down. Now sit in it. The action of sitting in the chair was faith or took faith (depending if you think of faith as a noun or verb). Belief that is so concrete that it inspires action and reliance. Now if we go back and analyze each time Jesus complimented or commented on someone's faith we see they are always linked to action.

The centurion who asked Jesus to heal his servant (Matthew 8:5-13), the Gentile woman who asked Jesus to heal her daughter (Matthew 15:21-28), the woman with the blood disease that touched the hem of Jesus' cloak(Mark 5:25-34), the men who lowered their friend through the roof to Jesus for healing (Luke 5:17-26) all had a belief held so deeply that it inspired action. It can even be seen in Jesus' rebuke of his disciples on the Sea of Galilee.

> [35]That day when evening came, he said to his disciples, Let us go over to the other side."[36]Leaving the crowd behind, they took him along, just as he was, in the boat. There were also other boats with him. [37]A furious squall came up, and the waves broke over the boat, so that it was nearly swamped. [38]Jesus was in the stern, sleeping on a cushion. The disciples woke him and said to him, Teacher, don't you care if we drown?"[39]He got up, rebuked the wind and said to the waves, Quiet! Be still!"Then the wind died down and it was completely calm. [40]He said to his disciples, "Why are you so afraid? Do you still have no faith? [41]They were terrified and asked each other, Who is this? Even the wind and the waves obey him!"

Mark 4:35-41

Keep in mind this is the criticism he leveled at men that had seen him heal the sick and open blind eyes. Their belief was undoubtedly strong but they didn't have it to the level where their actions supported it. When confronted with a seemingly insurmountable situation they didn't trust that God the father was good enough to protect themselves and Jesus. Instead they went to Jesus with questioning accusations and required immediate action. In this case, their faith did not run deep enough to inspire trust in God.

If we use this definition of faith we can see that Jesus was truly the pioneer of Faith. Let's review what Jesus prayed in the Garden of Gethsemane.

> "39Going a little farther, he fell with his face to the ground and prayed, "My Father, if it is possible, may this cup be taken from me. Yet not as I will, but as you will."
>
> *Matthew 26:39*

Even more personally inspiring is the fact that Jesus went back to God and requested the same thing again. This demonstrates that it is okay to petition God for things that we are not certain are in his will. Making the request is still God honoring as long as we subordinate our will to his. This should give us the faith to boldly request the true desires of our heart without concern for God's judgment of our wishes. As long as we are willing to follow God's path even if it doesn't lead to those desires (or maybe allowing God to change our desires) God will honor our prayer.

> "⁴²He went away a second time and
> prayed, "My Father, if it is not possible
> for this cup to be taken away unless I
> drink it, may your will be done."

Matthew 16:42

Those prayers clearly demonstrate that Jesus did not want to proceed down the path of crucifixion. He also clearly had faith that God's will was the correct path in the situation. Ultimately his belief in the goodness of his father led him to lay his life down, contrary to his own desires. His belief inspired an action that certainly constituted faith. The final confirmation of his faith can be seen in some of his last words on the cross.

> "⁴⁴It was now about noon, and darkness
> came over the whole land until three
> in the afternoon, ⁴⁵for the sun stopped
> shining. And the curtain of the temple
> was torn in two. ⁴⁶Jesus called out with
> a loud voice, "Father, into your hands I
> commit my spirit."When he had said this,
> he breathed his last."

Luke 23:44-46

But you might ask, "where is the faith in that?" Jesus was doing all the work in the crucifixion. He was ultimately returning to heaven which is his home, right? Why did he have to trust the father?

> ³²God has raised this Jesus to life,
> and we are all witnesses of it."

> *Acts 2:32*

....

It was not Jesus own power that raised him from the dead but his father's. Simply put Jesus had to have faith that his heavenly father would resurrect him from the grave. He had to be willing to submit to the punishment and pain of the cross that he knew would end in his death. His death. A condition he had now power to correct. He had to trust in father's will right up to the point of surrendering himself to purgatory and ultimately a stop in hell, a place he had no power to return from. He had to depend on his father for the resurrection that would free him from hell. That puts a whole new perspective on his statement in Luke.

> "Father, into your hands I commit my
> spirit."

> *Luke 23:46*

....

That is the ultimate step of faith. A step that every christian will need to take eventually and Jesus was the first to take it. That is why he is the pioneer of our faith. Did Jesus have faith?.... For the new testament christian he created it.

JUST A MUSTARD SEED

At this point you should be fairly certain of the necessity of faith and hopefully have a little different understanding of what it means. Now that we know we need it, how do we develop it? Scripture is very clear, all we need is faith the size of a mustard seed.

> [14]When they came to the crowd, a man approached Jesus and knelt before him. [15]"Lord, have mercy on my son," he said. "He has seizures and is suffering greatly. He often falls into the fire or into the water. [16]I brought him to your disciples, but they could not heal him."
>
> [17]"You unbelieving and perverse generation," Jesus replied, "how long shall I stay with you? How long shall I put up with you? Bring the boy here to me." [18]Jesus rebuked the demon, and it came out of the boy, and he was healed at that moment.
>
> [19]Then the disciples came to Jesus in private and asked, "Why couldn't we drive it out?"
>
> [20]He replied, "Because you have so little faith. Truly I tell you, if you have faith as small as a mustard seed, you can say to this mountain, 'Move from here to there,' and it will move. Nothing will be impossible for you."
>
> *Matthew 17:14-20*

What? If they have faith the size of a mustard seed they would be able to tell a mountain to move and it will move but their faith was too little to cast out the demon. Does that mean casting out demons is harder than moving a mountain with a request? That can't be true because the disciples had cast out demons before. Was this one special? This also seems to imply that all faith is not created equal. He describes their faith as "so little". If we think back to other times that Jesus commented on someone's faith he also seemed to insinuate that all faith was not created equal. Consider what he told the centurion.

> "10When Jesus heard this, he was amazed and said to those following him, Truly I tell you, I have not found anyone in Israel with such great faith.

Matthew 8:10

Clearly this faith was greater than what anyone had displayed to Jesus. That means faith is not a one size fits all item. It is something that comes in various different sizes. Let's look at the other scripture that references mustard seed faith.

> 5The apostles said to the Lord, "Increase our faith!" 6He replied, "If you have faith as small as a mustard seed, you can say to this mulberry tree, 'Be uprooted and planted in the sea,' and it will obey you."

Luke 17:5-6

Well that doesn't help. The apostles ask Jesus to increase their faith and he responds that a mustard seed is enough. That seems dismissive. The apostles, those closest to Jesus with the most first hand knowledge of his miracles, the ones he actually explained his parables to, all seem to think they need greater faith. Clearly there are different sizes of faith. Different levels we can strive for. But how can you need greater faith if a mustard seed is enough? Maybe the answer can be found in another parable that references a mustard seed.

> "³¹He told them another parable: "The kingdom of heaven is like a mustard seed, which a man took and planted in his field.³²Though it is the smallest of all seeds, yet when it grows, it is the largest of garden plants and becomes a tree, so that the birds come and perch in its branches."
>
> *Matthew 13: 31-32*

Perhaps that is what Christ intended when he said all we needed was the faith of a mustard seed. If we apply this parable to faith it means that we do in fact need just a mustard seed worth of faith but it does not mean that seed is to stay a seed. It needs to grow to be a tree so it can provide a perch for the birds and shade for others. A place of solace and rest. A mighty tree. This makes it much easier to understand why Jesus said it only takes faith the size of a mustard seed to move a mountain. Can faith the size of a mustard seed move the mountain, no probably not. It couldn't even cast out a demon. But a mustard seed worth of faith, with God's blessing, and time grows into a mighty tree that can cast mountains into the sea.

What does this mean for us today? What does it tell us about how we become effective prayer warriors? Simply put, you only need the tiniest statement of faith to start the journey. The belief that Jesus was the son of God and died for your sins. A belief that is so deep you are willing to surrender your life to him. A belief that makes you willing to act....Faith. That act of surrendering your life plants that seed of faith. Then, assuming the seed was planted in good soil, all we need is water, sunlight, and time to grow a mighty tree. It is this tree of faith that enables us to pray with greater power. As our faith increases so will the depth of our prayers and our willingness to act on the Lord's callings. As our tree grows God's power is more and more able to manifest on this earth through our actions and prayers. All from a mustard seed worth of faith that was planted, watered, and grown into a tree.

CHAPTER 5:

GROWING A TREE

A SEED IS ONLY POTENTIAL IF IT'S NOT PLANTED

If you're like most people then you're thinking, great: I'm called to have faith. It's critically important to my walk with God. I'm supposed to provide a seed but I can't let it stay a seed. If I'm to maximize my life's impact for God, it must develop into a tree. How the #$%@ do I grow a tree? When confused, turn to scripture. We've used this one earlier but let's revisit it in a different translation.

> ²Looking unto Jesus, the author and finisher of our faith,
>
> *Hebrews 12:2*

That's some good news. Jesus is the author and finisher of our faith. If he is responsible for starting, crafting, and finishing our faith that would seem that we have little to no responsibility for its development. This also appears to be confirmed in Ephesians.

> ⁸For it is by grace you have been saved, through faith—and this is not from yourselves, it is the gift of God—
>
> *Ephesians 2:8*

It's a gift. We may be responsible for the seed but God and Jesus, is responsible for growing it into a tree. But that doesn't make sense. If Jesus is responsible for crafting our faith then why did he criticize his disciples for not having enough? Remember what he said to them on the boat.

> ²⁶He replied, "You of little faith,
> why are you so afraid?"Then he got up and
> rebuked the winds and the waves, and it
> was completely calm.
>
> *Matthew 8:26*

Why would Jesus criticize them for something they have no control over? That doesn't seem to make sense at all. Again we are left with an apparent contradiction regarding faith. Since Jesus compared faith to a seed and since he so frequently used examples found in nature let's analyze faith using our previous tree analogy. What controls the growth of a tree? The amount of sunlight it receives, the amount of water it receives, and the quality of the soil. Perhaps our answers to what is needed to grow a tree of faith can be found in the same analogy.

THE SUNLIGHT

This principle is the most simplistic but also the least applied. A tree cannot create food and grow without photosynthesis. Rain and the nutrients from the soil are critical but they are useless to the tree without photosynthesis. Ironically, all it needs to do in order to do this is be in the presence of the light. Do you recall what the light was from chapter 1? Jesus. In order to grow a bigger tree we need to spend time in the presence of Jesus. This is such an important point it deserves an entire chapter just to unpack it. For now you will have to accept this at face value! We need to be in the presence of God. How do we do that?

⁸Come near to God and he will come
near to you.

James 4:8

....

THE WATER

Water is the lifeblood of a tree. Water is not actually
used in creating the food that a tree uses, instead, it is the
transportation system that moves nutrients within the
roots up to the leaves which use them in the process of
photosynthesis. This is the same way God uses the good
things he does in our life. The goodness and blessings of
God are a steady rain. This rain is critical to the growth
of our tree but it only benefits the tree if it's absorbed.
How do we "absorb" God's goodness and blessings? We
reflect on what he has done. It's been said that you can't
really figure out how to get where you're going if you don't
know where you've been. This is true in our walk with
God. We must take time to look at the things he's done
in our life and allow that to build our faith. This makes
perfect sense when you think about the concept of trust.
It is frequently said trust is not given its earned. It is by
trial and confirmation that we build a deep trust in the
goodness of God.

This is the point where we should give you a scripture
that clearly states reflecting on what God's done is critical
to faith. In researching reflection something stood out,
there isn't a scripture that says you should. What there is,
is a consistent theme that runs throughout the bible. The
theme of thanksgiving and praise. This is a bit puzzling.
The creator of the heavens and the earth, the being who

literally created every human, needs his creation to praise him? Is he really that shallow and narcissistic? Why does a being that is perfect in every way want or need to be worshiped, thanked, and praised? Perhaps the answer to this question is the very principle of reflection.

Consider thanksgiving. In order to be truly thankful you must have something to be thankful for. A true heart of thanksgiving requires you to reflect on something God has done for you in an attitude of appreciation. It would be difficult to discuss biblical thanksgiving without discussing David. He wrote many of the Psalms and did so in various states of turmoil, contentment, requesting and praise. If you spend some time skimming through them you will see a remarkable consistency. When David offers God thanks he does so with purpose. He very rarely uses generalities, instead choosing to make specific references to the good things God's done. Psalms 9 is a good example.

> [1]I will give thanks to you, Lord, with all my heart; I will tell of all your wonderful deeds. [2]I will be glad and rejoice in you; I will sing the praises of your name, O Most High. [3]My enemies turn back; they stumble and perish before you. [4]For you have upheld my right and my cause, sitting enthroned as the righteous judge. [5]You have rebuked the nations and destroyed the wicked; you have blotted out their name for ever and ever. [6]Endless ruin has overtaken my enemies, you have uprooted their cities; even the memory of them has perished.
>
> *Psalms 9 1-6*

Keep in mind, David was a king of Israel whose main purpose was to protect his people. What David did was wage war which makes the thanks he expressed very specific to things he sought God for. He reflected on his victories which caused him to approach God with an overwhelming attitude of Thanksgiving.

The other biblical justification for the need of reflection can be found in God's desire for praise from his people. The number of scriptures that instruct us to praise God is outstanding. It is a message that is dotted throughout both the new and old testaments. Much like thanksgiving it is impossible to honestly praise God without considering what he has done in your life. Psalms 105 expressly tells us to do just that.

> [1]Give praise to the Lord, proclaim his name; make known among the nations what he has done. [2]Sing to him, sing praise to him; tell of all his wonderful acts. [3]Glory in his holy name; let the hearts of those who seek the Lord rejoice. [4]Look to the Lord and his strength; seek his face always. [5]Remember the wonders he has done, his miracles, and the judgments he pronounced.
>
> *Psalms 105:1-5*

Perhaps the reason why God is so adamant about the need for thanksgiving and praise is not because he needs to hear us offer up those sacrifices but because he knows we can't honestly do them without reflecting on what he's done. Perhaps he's just asking us to reflect on what he's done so that it will cause our faith to grow. It is the faithfulness of God that truly builds our faith. The realization of the great and many things he's done for you. From the answering of a simple prayer about your finances to the inspiring story of healing that you were a part of praying for; it is all just water for your tree of faith. Every prayer answered. Every impossible disaster averted. Every time you stand in awe at the beauty of his creation. It is affirmation of the power of God and food for your faith. When we reflect on all the amazing things God has done the only reasonable response is thanksgiving and praise.

If we apply the concept that thanksgiving is reflection it brings a whole new depth to Philippians 4:6:

> ⁶Do not be anxious about anything, but in every situation, by prayer and petition, with thanksgiving, present your requests to God. ⁷And the peace of God, which transcends all understanding, will guard your hearts and your minds in Christ Jesus.
>
> *Philippians 4:6*

We are to present our every need and situation to God by prayer and petition, while remembering all the amazing things he's done for us in the past. Through this God can grant you a peace beyond all understanding. Such a simplistic concept but one we miss so frequently. How can we worry about anything when we know all the amazing things he's done for us in the past. This starts to offer some clarity on the apparent contradiction regarding whether God or us is responsible for building our faith. We are required to reflect on the good things God has done but God is still the one doing the good things. He is authoring our faith but we still have to read the book!

Reflection is the key to watering your tree.

Reflection: This is a powerful concept that should be put into our lives on a daily basis. Reflecting on what God has already done gives us FAITH he will do it again. It can be the best comfort in hard times. Let's practice this technique now. List some amazing things God has done for you in your life and the specific details. Did you know it was God moving at the time or did you only see the fingerprints of God when you look back at the situation and the end results? How does this give you strength to go through the next trial that life will throw at you?

_____

_____

_____

_____

_____

_____

_____

_____

_____

_____

_____

_____

_____

_____

THE SOIL

The quality of the soil is one of the most critical aspects that affects the rate of growth and size of the tree. Jesus used a parable regarding soil to demonstrate this exact principle. It is known as the parable of the sower and is found in three of the four gospels. For consistency's sake we will stick with Matthew.

> Then he told them many things in parables, saying: "A farmer went out to sow his seed.[4]As he was scattering the seed, some fell along the path, and the birds came and ate it up.[5]Some fell on rocky places, where it did not have much soil. It sprang up quickly, because the soil was shallow.[6]But when the sun came up, the plants were scorched, and they withered because they had no root.[7]Other seed fell among thorns, which grew up and choked the plants.[8]Still other seed fell on good soil, where it produced a crop—a hundred, sixty or thirty times what was sown.
>
> *Matthew 13: 3-8*

This happens to be one of the few parables that Jesus' explanation of the parable is also recorded.

> [18]"Listen then to what the parable of the sower means:[19]When anyone hears the message about the kingdom and does not understand it, the evil one comes

and snatches away what was sown in their heart. This is the seed sown along the path. [20]The seed falling on rocky ground refers to someone who hears the word and at once receives it with joy. [21]But since they have no root, they last only a short time. When trouble or persecution comes because of the word, they quickly fall away. [22]The seed falling among the thorns refers to someone who hears the word, but the worries of this life and the deceitfulness of wealth choke the word, making it unfruitful. [23]But the seed falling on good soil refers to someone who hears the word and understands it. This is the one who produces a crop, yielding a hundred, sixty or thirty times what was sown.

Matthew 13:18-23

Before we dig into the details of this analogy there are a couple of subtle points that should be noted. First, the seed referred to in this analogy is the truth regarding the divine nature and sacrifice of Jesus. Second, the soil is our heart. Both of these facts are clearly presented in verse 19 but it is critically important that we understand those two facts before we apply this parable. Belief in Jesus as our personal lord and Saviour is the seed and it must be planted in our heart to grow a tree of faith.

Let's be very clear, the condition of our heart is of the utmost importance to God. No matter how much you water it, a seed cast on hard packed ground will not grow.

This is the first of the seeds describe by Jesus. This seed never had a chance. It was purely feed for the enemy. A heart that is hard, impliable, unforgiving, and tough is not a soil that can yield a strong tree capable of producing a great harvest. This can be said no better than it was by Solomon.

> ²³Above all else, guard your heart, for everything you do flows from it
>
> *Proverbs 4:23*

So how do we prepare our heart and make sure it is soft? Ezekiel tells us that it isn't really our responsibility.

> ²⁶I will give you a new heart and put a new spirit in you; I will remove from you your heart of stone and give you a heart of flesh. ²⁷And I will put my Spirit in you and move you to follow my decrees and be careful to keep my law
>
> *Ezekiel 36:26-27*

Reflection: This one will take some processing. What type of soil would you classify your heart as? Is it the hard packed soil, the rocky soil, the soil with the weeds, or the productive soil? Why? Does it change from time to time? Why or why not?

_____

_____

_____

_____

_____

_____

_____

_____

_____

_____

_____

_____

_____

_____

Isn't that amazing?! Our hearts are a solid stone before he removes them and replaces them with a heart of flesh. It is impossible for the seed to find purchase prior to this. God gives a heart that is capable of receiving his word. To put it simply, God is in the heart business. This is even clearer when you apply what Jesus said regarding his yoke to this parable.

> [29]Take my yoke upon you and learn from me, for I am gentle and humble in heart, and you will find rest for your souls. [30]For my yoke is easy and my burden is light.
>
> *Matthew 11:29-30*

This statement from Jesus is one that plagues many Christians. They imagine Jesus as the kind farmer having us pull his plow along in the field. Perhaps something like this.

This isn't what he intended at all. Oxen worked in teams so when Jesus said his yoke was light he was referring to something like this.

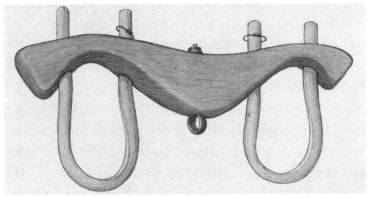

Jesus is telling us he is side by side with us pulling the plow that breaks up the soil of our heart. We aren't working alone, we are working with a partner! Just another example of why he is the perfecter of our faith.

The next condition of the soil is the one that seems to be the most transitional but also the most critical. Jesus describes this soil as rocky and shallow. In this soil the seed springs up quickly but the soil doesn't allow a good strong root system to be established. As the sun bakes the soil the tree withers and dies. We've all seen these people. They show up to church and immediately start serving at all the services. Every time you walk in the door they are there. They seem so on fire and passionate with their faith, then, they're just gone. Maybe they were offended by something someone said. Maybe the pastor preached one too many sermons on the importance of giving. Maybe lake season rolled back around... or baseball season... or football season. They have such a passionate fire but when it was time for the sustained sacrifice, the dry time, they wither and disappear.

How do we assure that this soil is not the condition of our hearts? Get the rocks out. These rocks tend to be the things that are the most ingrained in our being that we don't really enjoy dealing with. Many are personality traits or tendencies that have a deep foundation in how we respond to the world and to God. These are the things that cause you to believe you don't need God or that God doesn't need you. Maybe its pride, independence, lack of trust, laziness, lust, or lack of generosity. Maybe it's apathy, people pleasing, self medicating, or pleasure seeking. The stones in our soil are generally not temporary, nor are they situational. Identifying the stones in your heart is not easy work. It is painful and humbling but it is absolutely necessary for God to create a rich soil.

In order to identify the stones in our soil we must spend some time, with Jesus, sifting through the soil. Allow him to show you what's a rock that needs to be cast aside, what's a dirt clod that just needs to be watered and worked a little more and what's good clean fertile soil.

Analogies are great but how do we actually do this. Surprise, Surprise... we PRAY. Ask God to search your heart and show you what isn't good soil. The bible says that David was a man after God's own heart (1 Samuel 13:14) and this is what David had to say about his heart.

²³Search me, God, and know my heart;
test me and know my anxious thoughts.
²⁴See if there is any offensive way in me,
and lead me in the way everlasting.

Psalm 139: 23-24

....

A man that God himself described as after his own heart still needed to ask God to search his heart and reveal anything in him that was offensive. Really what David was saying was "God, help me get the rocks out".

Reflection: This may be the most painful reflection in the entire book but it will also be the most productive. What are the rocks in your soil? Some were listed in the paragraphs above but that list is far from comprehensive. What are the deep flaws that keep you from being productive for God? Remember, these are not temporary, situational, fleeting things. These are the things that you keep dealing with. If you can't identify any, spend time praying David's prayer above. Don't glaze over this and make sure to fill it out even if you can't do it now. What are your rocks?

_____

_____

_____

_____

_____

_____

_____

_____

_____

_____

_____

The last example of unproductive soil is probably the most concerning and frankly the hardest to prevent. The soil that is grown up with thorns. Jesus described the thorns as the worries of this life and the deceitfulness of wealth. The Gospel of Luke describes them as the "life's worries, riches and pleasures". These are the temporary and situational things that distract us from God's calling. What's most telling about this description is the breadth of things that fall into this category. It's all of life's normal concerns and worries like who is my kid hanging out with, what does that special someone think of me, or even that cancer diagnosis a family member got last week. But it's also all the wants and distractions of wealth. This can be planning that next vacation or that next big purchase. It can be plotting your career path or grinding at work trying to get ahead and make that little bit more. Maybe it's obsessing about that new car, boat, or house. The one that will finally satisfy you. Jesus was clear about God's expectations of how we should handle our daily concerns.

²⁵"Therefore I tell you, do not worry about your life, what you will eat or drink; or about your body, what you will wear. Is not life more than food, and the body more than clothes? ²⁶Look at the birds of the air; they do not sow or reap or store away in barns, and yet your heavenly Father feeds them. Are you not much more valuable than they? ²⁷Can any one of you by worrying add a single hour to your life? ²⁸"And why do you worry about clothes? See how the flowers of the eld grow. They do not labor or spin. ²⁹Yet I tell you that not even Solomon in all his splendor was dressed like one of these. ³⁰If that is how God clothes the grass of the field, which is here today and tomorrow is thrown into the fire, will he not much more clothe you—you of little faith? ³¹So do not worry, saying, 'What shall we eat?' or 'What shall we drink?' or 'What shall we wear?' ³²For the pagans run after all these things, and your heavenly Father knows that you need them. ³³But seek first his kingdom and his righteousness, and all these things will be given to you as well. ³⁴Therefore do not worry about tomorrow, for tomorrow will worry about itself. Each day has enough trouble of its own.

Matthew 6:25-34

....

That is easy to say but very hard to do. If we are honest then most of us would say that we can't really not worry about what we would eat tomorrow. If we did that then we wouldn't ever go to work and we would starve, right?

Are we really just supposed to trust God to provide what we need? The answer to this confusion can be found in the same verse from Philippians we discussed earlier.

> ⁶Do not be anxious about anything, but in every situation, by prayer and petition, with thanksgiving, present your requests to God. ⁷And the peace of God, which transcends all understanding, will guard your hearts and your minds in Christ Jesus.
>
> *Philippians 4:6-7*

In this verse is the key. It's not that we are supposed to ignore the things that worry us. It's that we are to take those things to God in prayer. It is through this prayer that God will grant us the peace that is necessary for us to truly stop worrying. It's not that we are called not to worry, just that we are called to turn our worries over to God. Hold those thoughts captive. The best analogy for this is a bird flying over your head. You can't prevent a bird from flying over your head but you can stop it from making a nest in your hair. It is the same with our worries and concerns. We can't honestly prevent a worry from developing but we can immediately take that worry to God and leave it with him. Stop dwelling on it and trust God. Don't let it make a nest in your hair!

The other part of the thorns is the deceitfulness of wealth. This is a very controversial topic among Christians. Are we supposed to be poor and give all our money away or will God bless us and provide us with more? Is it a prosperity or a poverty Gospel? Who draws the line on what is poor and rich? As an example, take a moment and ask a kid under the age of 10 what is a crazy big amount of money. If you live in the US they will probably say $50 or $100. Then ask a 15 or 16 year old. Your answers will likely fall in the $1,000 to $5,000 range. Now answer the question yourself. $10,000, $50,000, $100,000? Who's right, the adult because they have more experience? But what about the fact that Jesus said?

> ²He called a little child to him, and placed the child among them. ³And he said: "Truly I tell you, unless you change and become like little children, you will never enter the kingdom of heaven.
>
> *Matthew 18:2-3*

Let's be perfectly clear. If you are reading this book it is almost certain that you are rich. Jesus didn't just come for the western cultures he came for everyone. Your wealth must be compared to that of the human population as a whole. Do you know you will have money for food tomorrow? You're rich. Do you own a car? You're rich. Do you own a house? You're extravagantly rich. Now that you have the proper perspective let's look at what Jesus said about wealth in the Gospel of Mark.

¹⁷As Jesus started on his way, a man ran up to him and fell on his knees before him. "Good teacher,"he asked, what must I do to inherit eternal life?"¹⁸"Why do you call me good?"Jesus answered."No one is good—except God alone. ¹⁹You know the commandments: You shall not murder, you shall not commit adultery, you shall not steal, you shall not give false testimony, you shall not defraud, honor your father and mother."²⁰"Teacher,"he declared, all these I have kept since I was a boy." ²¹Jesus looked at him and loved him. "One thing you lack,"he said. "Go, sell everything you have and give to the poor, and you will have treasure in heaven. Then come, follow me." ²²At this the man's face fell. He went away sad, because he had great wealth. ²³Jesus looked around and said to his disciples, "How hard it is for the rich to enter the kingdom of God!" ²⁴The disciples were amazed at his words. But Jesus said again, Children, how hard it is to enter the kingdom of God! ²⁵It is easier for a camel to go through the eye of a needle than for someone who is rich to enter the kingdom of God."

Mark 10:17-25

That is a pretty damning statement. That should clarify what we are supposed to do, we are to give it all away and be poor. Until you read the next verse.

> ²⁶The disciples were even more amazed,
> and said to each other, "Who then can be
> saved?" ²⁷Jesus looked at them and said,
> "With man this is impossible, but not
> with God; all things are possible with
> God."
>
> *Mark 10:26-27*

If you step back and read that it's actually a little funny. The disciples heard what Jesus said and they all got a little nervous. Jesus' statements were so demanding they started wondering whether they were going to make the cut. In analyzing Jesus' response let's start with one important fact, apparently it was not a problem that the rich young ruler was rich. In fact, if you look at verse 21 he is one of a hand full of people that scripture specifically states that Jesus loved. He loved him so much he actually called him to be a disciple. What an honor! The problem is that when he was offered one of the greatest opportunities in history, the chance to follow Jesus, the loss of his great wealth made him sad. Perhaps what Jesus was trying to say is that with money comes risks to the condition of your heart. You've most likely heard it quoted that "money is the root of all evil". That is actually in the bible but the quote isn't quite right.

> ¹⁰For the love of money is a root of
> all kinds of evil. Some people, eager for
> money, have wandered from the faith and
> pierced themselves with many griefs.
>
> *1 Timothy 6:10*

That certainly seems to agree with what happened with the rich young ruler. His love of his money caused him to wander away from his faith. So how do we assure we don't follow the path of the rich young ruler and let the weeds grow up in our soil?

The best way to weed your soil is to approach anything you have with the following mentality. I didn't earn it, I don't deserve it, and (most importantly) I can't keep it.

If you are able to truly internalize this statement it will be like round up for the weeds in your soil. We must approach everything that we have with a spirit of humility understanding that we didn't "earn" anything. You might believe that you worked hard and built that company from the ground up but do you realize that God gave you the ability to do that work and sent those clients and customers your way. You might believe that you buckled down and earned that degree but do you realize your intelligence and wisdom is a gift from God? You might believe that you consistently sacrifice for your family and that is why you have such great kids or such a great marriage. Do you realize that it is God that grants you the wisdom to see those areas that you can serve and gives you a heart willing to do so. Does that irritate your pride? Do you think you earned what you have?

> [17]Every good and perfect gift is from above, coming down from the Father of the heavenly lights, who does not change like shifting shadows.
>
> *James 1:17*

Hurt your pride some? How about this?

> ⁶All of us have become like one who is unclean, and all our righteous acts are like filthy rags; we all shrivel up like a leaf, and like the wind our sins sweep us away.
>
> *Isaiah 64:6*

Your good works, your effort, your hustle, is nothing but a gift and a gift you don't deserve. A deep internal belief in this fact means it's unreasonable to cling to money.

The most critical part of the mindset is really the most simplistic. If we didn't earn it and we don't deserve it then how can we possibly hope to keep it. If it was a gift from God then how can we demand that he continue providing it? If someone gave you a Christmas gift of a AAA membership for a year should you expect them to continue to pay for it the next year? Put simply, we can't keep it. Your marriage, your finances, your job, your children, your health. Everything we have that is good and valuable is a gift that relies on God's grace to keep it in our lives. I didn't earn it, I don't deserve it, and I can't keep it. If the rich young ruler had applied this mindset we'd likely be discussing the thirteenth disciple!

The progressive nature of the parable of the soil is astounding when you look at it wholistically. Jesus is really describing the process every follower of Christ must go through to yield a heart that is acceptable to God. Your heart is not just one of these conditions.

At some point in time it will or has been all of them. This is not a one and done process either. Does a farmer only till the soil once or does he need to continue to break up the soil to keep it from becoming hard packed and choking out the crops. Does a farmer just pick the weeds once or does he have to be ever vigilant of them growing up in the field and choking out the harvest. As the topsoil is softened rocks will work their way to the surface and we will need to spend time sifting through our soil to remove them. Fortunately Jesus is yoked with us and both of us are tending the soil of his harvest. Even better, he is doing most of the work and our burden is light!

One important final note. Jesus made it very clear that all good soils are not the same.

> ²³This is the one who produces a crop, yielding a hundred, sixty or thirty times what was sown.
>
> *Matthew 13:23*

With that in mind how do we improve the quality of our soil so our tree can grow larger and produce a greater yield? Fertilize. Every scripture, every sermon, every bible study, every conversation with a fellow believer and every prayer are amendments to your soil that will improve its chemistry and productivity for the kingdom. The next few chapters are practical application chapters that focus on improving the quality of your soil and maximizing the potential harvest from your tree.

Remember, increasing your faith increases the size of your hose and makes you a more effective conduit of God's power so it is imperative that we improve the soil.

....

"I am the true vine, and my Father is the gardener. ²He cuts off every branch in me that bears no fruit, while every branch that does bear fruit he prunes so that it will be even more fruitful. ³You are already clean because of the word I have spoken to you. ⁴Remain in me, as I also remain in you. No branch can bear fruit by itself; it must remain in the vine. Neither can you bear fruit unless you remain in me. ⁵"I am the vine; you are the branches. If you remain in me and I in you, you will bear much fruit; apart from me you can do nothing. ⁶If you do not remain in me, you are like a branch that is thrown away and withers; such branches are picked up, thrown into the fire and burned. ⁷If you remain in me and my words remain in you, ask whatever you wish, and it will be done for you. ⁸This is to my Father's glory, that you bear much fruit, showing yourselves to be my disciples.

John 5:1-8

....

CHAPTER 6:

BEING THE LIGHT

SOMETIMES ALL YOU NEED TO DO IS BE THERE

One of the most confusing aspects of Christianity is the necessity that you develop a relationship with someone you can't see, hear, or touch. People tell us, "You just need more Jesus" or " You need to spend more time with God" but never define what that means. How do we get more of something we can't touch? How do we spend time with someone we can't see or hear? This chapter establishes several simple (but not easy) action steps that allow you to get and remain in the light and close to Jesus.

1# DAILY BIBLE READING

At the risk of being trite, daily reading of the Bible is the single most transformative discipline that a christian can develop. Test it. List the three "most Christian" people you admire and ask them how often they read the Bible. Then ask them how important they think the reading habit is. You will be amazed at the results. This leads us to the question: Why is daily reading so transformational? Why does reading the word of God transform us or is that concept wrong and it doesn't really change us at all? To unpack daily bible reading we need to embrace a rather odd verse.

> [14]The Word became flesh and made his dwelling among us. We have seen his glory, the glory of the one and only Son, who came from the Father, full of grace and truth.
>
> *John 1:14*

Based on this scripture we see that Jesus and the word are one in the same. If that is true then when we read our Bible we are spending time with Jesus, by definition. This fact may show us that Bible reading is demonstrably spending time with Jesus but that does not explain why it is transformational or necessary. If we look to Jesus' words we can see a more explicit requirement for Bible reading.

> [7]If you remain in me and my words remain in you, ask whatever you wish, and it will be done for you. [8]This is to my Father's glory, that you bear much fruit, showing yourselves to be my disciples.
>
> *John 15:7-8*

When we apply the knowledge that Jesus is the word of God we see a mandate from Christ.

If you remain in **the word** and my words remain in you, ask whatever you wish, and it will be done for you. This is to my Father's glory, that you bear much fruit, showing yourselves to be my disciples.

Reading the Bible daily allows you to "bear much fruit" and is how we show ourselves to by Christ's disciples. A mandate from Jesus to read the Bible. Psalms 119 further summarizes the importance of bible reading.

103How sweet are your words to my
taste, sweeter than honey to my mouth! 104I
gain understanding from your precepts;
therefore I hate every wrong path. 105Your
word is a lamp for my feet, a light on
my path.

Psalm 119:103-105

....

9How can a young person stay on the
path of purity? By living according to
your word. 10I seek you with all my heart;
do not let me stray from your commands.
11I have hidden your word in my heart that
I might not sin against you.

Psalm 119:11

....

Daily Bible reading teaches us God's will, purpose, and desires for our life. In a sense it's his instruction manual for living in this world. With that in mind it seems obvious that we can't hope to know what God's expectations of us are if we don't read the directions. What's more impressive is that hiding the word in our heart is actually part of the process to turning from sin. When we have the truths of God in our hearts and gain a true understanding of the character of God it allows us to more effectively avoid the allure of sin. In fact, it is reading the bible, the law, that shows us what is sin and what isn't.

²⁰The law was brought in so that the
trespass might increase….

Romans 5:20

....

That is a pretty confounding statement. One of the things that frustrates so many people when they begin to study the Bible is the fact that it is rarely explicit. The bible doesn't just lay out what we should or shouldn't do in a convenient list of daily, weekly, monthly and yearly expectations. It doesn't even give us many direct commandments (at least few that Jesus didn't seem to upend). We don't like that it is not neat and tidy. Simple and straightforward. The truth is that if it was simple and straightforward it wouldn't be very relevant most of the time.

The Bible was written thousands of years ago in an agricultural economy where the wheel and aqueduct where technological marvels. How can a book be written in such a way that millenia later it still has application in today's world? The answer is by using parables and stories that demonstrate principles. By telling historical stories that show the heart of God in action. If you are wanting to explain who God is and what he desires then shouldn't you do so by discussing what he's done through his followers? This is why the Bible is so abstract. It teaches us the truths of God and gives us the best information we have on his character and desires. Simply put we can't hope to know God and get closer to him if we don't read his biography.

While knowledge of God is a clear benefit of daily Bible reading there is a much deeper truth in Psalm 119. Daily Bible reading gives opportunity for God to speak directly to us and is a vehicle for the Holy Spirit to move within us.

The odds are you don't know anybody who has heard the audible voice of God but the odds are equally high that you do know multiple people that would say God spoke to them through a scripture or verse. How is this possible?

> [12]For the word of God is alive and active. Sharper than any double-edged sword, it penetrates even to dividing soul and spirit, joints and marrow; it judges the thoughts and attitudes of the heart.
>
> *Hebrews 4:12*

God's word is alive. It speaks directly to us in the moment. It brings the comfort, guidance, and peace of God directly to our hearts. In the hectic dog eat dog world we live in there are thousands of things vying for our attention and focus. Distractions are the rule not the exception. Reading the Bible daily creates a daily opportunity for God to speak directly to us. The importance of this can't be understated. Hoping to hear from God but not reading your Bible daily is like trying to have a conversation with someone at a concert... standing in front of the speakers...with earplugs in. It may not be impossible but it is certainly going to take longer, be more prone to error and cause frustration.

Two more scriptures shed light on an additional benefit of daily bible reading. This benefit is often overlooked but should not be missed.

> ²but whose delight is in the law of the Lord, and who meditates on his law day and night. 3That person is like a tree planted by streams of water, which yields its fruit in season and whose leaf does not wither whatever they do prospers.
>
> *Psalm 1:2-3*

....

> ⁸Keep this Book of the Law always on your lips; meditate on it day and night, so that you may be careful to do everything written in it. Then you will be prosperous and successful.
>
> *Joshua 1:8*

....

Pretty explicit. Bible reading is the beginning of God prospering you. This truth is far more complicated than a simple statement like this and deserves a much deeper discussion so we will revisit it later in this chapter.

So, that's the Why of daily Bible reading but there are several good methods of applying this truth. Below is a quick summary of three techniques for daily reading.

READING PLANS AND
DEVOTIONALS WITH FRIENDS

> ²⁰For where two or three gather in my
> name, there am I with them."
>
> *Matthew 18:20*

....

Reading a plan alongside a group of friends allows God to more effectively enter into the reading time. You don't have to read together or even at the same time. Just read the same thing. When you do this conversations will be sparked that will further your understanding and curiosity. When you gather together, Jesus will show up.

STUDYING FOR SOMETHING YOU
ARE STRUGGLING WITH

> ¹⁶All Scripture is God-breathed and is
> useful for teaching, rebuking, correcting
> and training in righteousness, ¹⁷so that
> the servant of God may be thoroughly
> equipped for every good work.
>
> *2 Timothy 3:16-17*

....

When you are struggling with a decision or issue find a bible reading plan that deals with that issue. Google search Bible verses that deal with it. Oftentimes incredibly relevant answers are ready and available but we just need to look.

BIBLE IN A YEAR

> [1]In the past God spoke to our ancestors through the prophets at many times and in various ways, [2]but in these last days he has spoken to us by his Son, whom he appointed heir of all things, and through whom also he made the universe. [3]The Son is the radiance of God's glory and the exact representation of his being, sustaining all things by his powerful word. After he had provided purification for sins, he sat down at the right hand of the Majesty in heaven.

Hebrews 1:1-3

Pick a bible plan that has you read every word of the bible in 365 days. This method of reading has you take in the full breadth of the Lord's word and is the beginning of hiding it in your heart. This type of reading will sometimes seem like a grind. It will also strengthen your faith when you find an answer to an active issue you are having hiding within your daily reading. Think about it, God was so good and so smart that he planned to have that very answer you needed ready and waiting before you ever needed it.

This is a very personal truth for me. In the process of writing this book my mother passed away. Mom had been battling stage four breast cancer that metastasized to her bones for nearly 5 years. It came time to stop treatment and place her on hospice care.

The very day Mom was placed on hospice a client of mine called me with a pretty big issue. I didn't have the time or energy to talk with him so I avoided his calls and texts for about 4 days (in my defense he started calling on a Friday).

When I did call him back he explained that he had heard about my mother and his father had recently passed. He went on to tell me 1 Corinthians 15 was a really powerful chapter for him.

He told me that maybe I should read that chapter and maybe even read it with my Mom. This was the only scripture anyone mentioned to me as we went through the process of Mom passing away. The next day I was reading my Bible in a year plan and I realized I was in the beginning of the book of 1 Corinthians. I honestly thought, "Oh I see what you're doing here God. This is going to be a comfort to me when she dies.", to be honest, God speaks to me so often like this I put it away and went on.

Fast forward to Saturday April 24th, my Mother takes a turn for the worst. I'm talking with my sister and I tell her this story regarding 1 Corinthians 15. I go on to tell her I realized that was on my daily reading list for Monday and I didn't think Mom had long left. I decided to take my clients advice and I read that chapter to my barely responsive mother that morning.

⁵³For the perishable must clothe itself
with the imperishable, and the mortal
with immortality. ⁵⁴When the perishable
has been clothed with the imperishable,
and the mortal with immortality, then the
saying that is written will come true:
"Death has been swallowed up in victory."

⁵⁵"Where, O death, is your victory?

Where, O death, is your sting?"

⁵⁶The sting of death is sin, and the
power of sin is the law. ⁵⁷But thanks be
to God! He gives us the victory through
our Lord Jesus Christ.

1 Corinthians 15:53-57

What I didn't know at the time was my sister was reading along with her kids in the other room. On Monday April 27th my Mom went home to God. My sister and her kids were the ones who walked in to find she had passed, which was the very situation she had been dreading. When I got to her house the only thing she could say was. "It was really peaceful. I'm surprised I'm not really upset by this. It's kind of just ok. Death, where is your string, right?" That's when I found out she had read along with me and that vey scripture was the one God used to comfort her at that time. Below is a screen clip of my daily bible in a year reading plan on the day my mother passed away.

Think about it. 296 days before my mother passed away God knew what was going to happen and made it so that scripture would be in my reading on that very day. Talk about seeing God move!

Reading the whole Bible in a year gives God the opportunity to create masterful coincidences!

#2 SERVING OTHERS

Jesus was very clear that for his followers service was not optional it is required. His response to James and John's request to be placed in seats of honor within his kingdom was incredibly pointed.

> "[42]Jesus called them together and said, "You know that those who are regarded as rulers of the Gentiles lord it over them, and their high officials exercise authority over them. [43]Not so with you. Instead, whoever wants to become great among you must be your servant, [44]and whoever wants to be first must be slave of all. [45]For even the Son of Man did not come to be served, but to serve, and to give his life as a ransom for many.
>
> *Mark 10:42-45*

Peter, in 1 Peter, was clear that the gifts we have been given, our talents, time, and treasure, are expected to be used to serve others.

> [10]Each of you should use whatever gift you have received to serve others, as faithful stewards of God's grace in its various forms.
>
> *1 Peter 4:10*

This calling is greater than just an expectation, it's an outright requirement. We are required to steward the resources given to us by our father specifically for the purpose of serving others. Service is literally the purpose of our spiritual gifts.

We again find an explicit requirement for us to do something without much explanation regarding why we should serve or what actually constitutes service. It's an intriguing question. Define Biblical service. Is it only working within the church or does it count the things we do individually outside of the church? Can it be for an organization or does it have to be for a specific entity?

Reflection: Write out a definition of service as required by the Bible. Be specific but resist the urge to use examples. Remember, a definition must encompass all the examples of service that you can think of. If it doesn't then your definition is incomplete or inaccurate.

_____

_____

_____

_____

_____

_____

_____

_____

_____

_____

_____

_____

_____

_____

Was that more difficult than you thought? Like Faith this seems to be something we should have a good grip on but for some reason we don't. Below is the definition we propose for service.

Service: Anything you do for another person that has nothing to do with your desires.

This definition makes determining if an activity is a service dependent on *why* you are doing something, not on *what* you're doing. This agrees with many scriptures but none more specific than the words of Jesus.

> ¹"Be careful not to practice your righteousness in front of others to be seen by them. If you do, you will have no reward from your Father in heaven.
>
> *Matthew 6:1*

To be clear this doesn't mean you have to hate what you're doing in order for it to be service. The truth is quite the opposite. God builds us for specific acts and services. Part of that construction often includes creating the desire in us to do those very things. With time we find that the work is actually the reward. This is the truly amazing thing about service, it is not just for those who are being served. As we serve those around us we begin to experience the joy of being used by God. It's certainly not always easy. It will often be hard, nerve racking, sacrificial, and at times painful. In order to serve as God intended, the service must truly not be about you but about others. Your needs, desires and wants must be put second to those you are serving. It's always humbling but the rewards are nearly indescribable.

> [18]This is what I have observed to be good: that it is appropriate for a person to eat, to drink and to find satisfaction in their toilsome labor under the sun during the few days of life God has given them— for this is their lot. [19]Moreover, when God gives someone wealth and possessions, and the ability to enjoy them, to accept their lot and be happy in their toil—this is a gift of God. [20]They seldom reflect on the days of their life, because God keeps them occupied with gladness of heart.

> *Ecclesiastes 5:18-20*

As we use our gifts for their intended purpose we point others to God and bring others into a closer relationship with him. Ironically this is the very purpose for which God sent Jesus to earth, to bring man into a relationship with him. As we serve others we are performing the very act that Christ performed. Like all things in life the more you do an act the more it begins to change you. To put it simply as we serve others we begin to be conformed into the image of Christ. As we are conformed to his image we become not only more effective at carrying out our father's will but also become closer to the father. The process of doing the work creates and strengthens the very relationship the father desires to have with us.

The consequences of that relationship deepening are the fruit of the spirit, Love, Joy, Peace, Patience, Kindness, Goodness, Faithfulness, Gentleness, and Self Control. Fruit that God then expects to be used to serve others.

Using the definition above you above there appears to be two distinctive types of service. Neither is more important than the other but we often focus on one to the detriment of the other.

SERVING AS EVANGELISM

Jesus was very specific with his disciples before he ascended into heaven.

> [18]Then Jesus came to them and said, "All authority in heaven and on earth has been given to me.[19]Therefore go and make disciples of all nations, baptizing them in the name of the Father and of the Son and of the Holy Spirit,[20]and teaching them to obey everything I have commanded you. And surely I am with you always, to the very end of the age."
>
> *Matthew 28:18-20*

That is our job. To go into all the world and let them know about the love of God. We are called to not only tell them about this love but to also demonstrate that love to them. Oftentimes we are called to be the hands of the feet of God. So that when they see us they see him. This type of service that people think of when they think of the Church.

Acts that show the love of God to those who don't know him. Acts that shine a light and make it so people want to see what is different about that person. Jesus described this very eloquently in Matthew.

> [14]"You are the light of the world. A town built on a hill cannot be hidden. [15]Neither do people light a lamp and put it under a bowl. Instead they put it on its stand, and it gives light to everyone in the house. [16]In the same way, let your light shine before others, that they may see your good deeds and glorify your Father in heaven.

Matthew 5:14-16

....

Unfortunately many Christians look at this type of service as the job of the church not the individuals in the church. This couldn't be farther from the truth. Jesus was very specific about this.

> [34] "A new command I give you: Love one another. As I have loved you, so you must love one another. [35]By this everyone will know that you are my disciples, if you love one another."

John 13:34-35

....

Jesus didn't make this optional. He said each of us was responsible for showing the love of God and it is only through this that we demonstrate we are his disciples.

Simply put if you are not serving those outside the church, sacrificially, you are falling short of your calling. When we serve in the church and as the church we demonstrate the love of God. When done correctly this brings people to him and makes them more cognizant of him.

> [11]You will be enriched in every way so that you can be generous on every occasion, and through us your generosity will result in thanksgiving to God.
>
> *2 Corinthians 9:11*

SERVING TO BUILD OTHERS UP

This type of service seems to be more overlooked by people. This is when people serve the Church within the church. The Bible is explicit about this type of service.

> [11]So Christ himself gave the apostles, the prophets, the evangelists, the pastors and teachers, [12]to equip his people for works of service, so that the body of Christ may be built up
>
> *Ephesians 4:11-12*

The misconception about this comes from the fact that few people consider themselves, pastors, teachers, apostles or prophets. People often think this is a type of service that others are called to do but certainly not themselves. After all they are school teachers, fire fighters, construction workers, and accountants. They aren't "given by Christ".

The book of Acts describes how the early church functioned. It describes how the gathered grew and cared for each other. It's something we don't often consider. When the disciples started the church there was no church to start. No Bible to read, no sermons from other pastors, no kids curriculum, and no church structure. All they knew was they needed to tell about Jesus and live the example of service that he lived. Acts tells us something staggering about that early church.

> [33]With great power the apostles continued to testify to the resurrection of the Lord Jesus. And God's grace was so powerfully at work in them all [34]that there were no needy persons among them. For from time to time those who owned land or houses sold them, brought the money from the sales [35]and put it at the apostles' feet, and it was distributed to anyone who had need.
>
> *Acts 4:33-35*

That's amazing. There were no needy among them. They took care of their own and made sure all had what was needed. The early church wasn't composed of full time pastors and lay members, it was composed of people from all walks of life that came together to meet each other's needs. What is staggering about this is that they did it without a Bible to lead them. They depended on the Holy Spirit to reveal God's desires. As one person learned something about God they brought it to the church and discussed it. The apostles went around planting seeds but they did not do the job of administering the church.

> [1]In those days when the number of disciples was increasing, the Hellenistic Jews among them complained against the Hebraic Jews because their widows were being overlooked in the daily distribution of food. [2]So the Twelve gathered all the disciples together and said, "It would not be right for us to neglect the ministry of the word of God in order to wait on tables. 3Brothers and sisters, choose seven men from among you who are known to be full of the Spirit and wisdom. We will turn this responsibility over to them 4and will give our attention to prayer and the ministry of the word."
>
> *Acts 6:1-3*

The funny thing about this type of service was it created an evangelical movement. Others saw a group of people coming together for food and fellowship. The sold property to meet needs and gave generously. When they saw this they couldn't help to wonder what made them so different. They saw how amazing it was and had to figure out how to become a part of it. Their internal service brought others to God.

#3 OBEDIENCE

Obedience is a very tough topic to address but it is one of the more foundational concepts of staying near to Jesus. Honestly it is the key to effectively implementing steps one and two. The necessity for obedience can't be more clearly put than what Jesus said in the book of John.

> "Those who accept my commandments and obey them are the ones who love me. And because they love me, my Father will love them. And I will love them and reveal myself to each of them."
>
> *John 14:21*

If we wish to know Jesus and understand who he is we must accept his commandments and obey them. He will reveal himself to us in the process. Through our obedience we will begin to truly understand Christ and by extension God the Father. But that isn't all he had to say about obedience.

> "If you love me, keep my commands. And I will ask the Father, and he will give you another advocate to help you and be with you forever—the Spirit of truth. The world cannot accept him, because it neither sees him nor knows him. But you know him, for he lives with you and will be in you."
>
> *John 14:15-17*

That's a pretty heavy statement. If you love Jesus you will keep his commandments and if you keep his commandments he will send you the advocate to be with you forever. It is our obedience to Christ that enables us to receive the spirit. This is not a statement of legalism. You are not saved by your works but we do need to attempt to walk the same path Jesus walked. That brings us to the most fundamental question. What did Jesus command? Interestingly enough there was a Pharisee that asked this very question of Jesus.

> [34]Hearing that Jesus had silenced the Sadducees, the Pharisees got together. [35]One of them, an expert in the law, tested him with this question: [36]"Teacher, which is the greatest commandment in the Law?" [37]Jesus replied:"Love the Lord your God with all your heart and with all your soul and with all your mind.' [38]This is the first and greatest commandment. [39]And the second is like it: "Love your neighbor as yourself.' [40]All the Law and the Prophets hang on these two commandments."
>
> *Matthew 22:34-40*

That makes it much more clear why following Jesus' command was a requirement of receiving the spirit. You must believe in and love both Jesus and God. This is the very statement of faith that we make when we become Christians. We may not perfectly execute it but we must believe it. He further confirms this in John.

"Jesus replied, "Anyone who loves me
will obey my teaching. My Father will
love them, and we will come to them and
make our home with them."

John 14:23

Obedience allows God to dwell with you.

These scriptures may clearly show that obedience is necessary to follow Christ but they certainly don't make it any easier to do. What does Obedience mean? Are we supposed to follow every commandment in the Old Testament? Do those rules still apply under the new covenant? What happens when we fail? Jesus said love God and love others, rights? What does that truly look like?

Reflection: What does obedience mean to you? Following the letter of the law? Just doing what's right? Is it only relevant toward your interaction with others or is there a deeper level of obedience to God? Define the general concept then define what it means as it relates to God. Give specific examples of things you are supposed to do and be honest about whether you do them.

_____

_____

_____

_____

_____

_____

_____

_____

_____

_____

_____

_____

_____

_____

_____

Think back to your childhood when your older sibling, parent or teacher told you not to do something that you knew you were capable of doing. What did you do? Odds are you that you at least considered bucking the system and doing what you wanted; and not what you were told. If you didn't trust the person or if the rule seemed too strict you were even more likely to defy the authority and do what you wanted to anyway. The more strict the rules the more likely we are to defy them. But why? Why are we naturally so averse to rules? Why do we have rules anyways? The bible offers us some answers. Lets look at a scripture from earlier.

> "Sin spread when the Law was given. But where sin spread, God's loving-favor spread all the more."

Romans 5:20

So God gave us rules so that sin would spread? That makes no sense. Why would he cause sin? Did the rules change anything that the Israelites were doing? Did they suddenly start coveting their neighbor's possessions when Moses came down from the mountain? Was it only after the commandments that they started to murder? We know that's not the case. So what did it mean that sin spread when the law was given? Perhaps he means that now they were on notice that it was sin. He told them the rule so now they chose whether to follow. The knowledge causes sin to spread because now people were making the choice to break the rule. So why have rules if they cause sin to multiple? Is it because God wants us to prove our love for him by following the rules?

> [22]But Samuel replied: "Does the Lord delight in burnt offerings and sacrifices as much as in obeying the Lord? To obey is better than sacrifice, and to heed is better than the fat of rams.
>
> *1 Samuel 15:22*

So that tells us that he doesn't desire obedience out of a desire for our sacrifice because he desires it more than sacrifice. Why is that so important? Because if God doesn't give us the rules out of a desire for sacrifice then there must be another purpose. He's not just telling us to do things because he wants to see if we will listen and follow the rules. That's just sacrifice. There has to be something more. The true purpose. The real purpose goes back to the proper perspective of God in relation to us. It is our wise father explaining how things work. Sometimes it is to prevent us from hurting ourselves, like a parent telling a child not to touch a hot stove. These are the more easily understandable instructions, but there are others that are more subtle and nuanced. Never cease in praying. Seek him daily in the word. Don't forget to come together with your church. Things that have a much deeper and more complicated meaning. Let's look to other scripture for a purpose to obedience.

> [33]Walk in obedience to all that the
> Lord your God has commanded you, so that
> you may live and prosper and prolong your
> days in the land that you will possess.
>
> *Deuteronomy 5:33*

....

It's God's commandments that lead us to prosperity and abundance. A good analogy would be to imagine God as a coach. A couch teaches you how to play the game. At first he is telling us the rules of the game so that we can keep from getting a penalty, a natural consequence to the action. These are the directions that are the easiest to understand; the most self explanatory. Don't lie, don't steal, don't kill. The obvious things that have clear cut consequences. As we work with God more he begins to tell us more subtle nuances about how to play the game. How to truly win. How to enjoy the game instead of making it a grind. As we begin to trust his instruction we start applying his directions. We get better at the game and as we get better he teaches us new techniques thus making us more successful at the game. The concept of learned obedience is further supported by the fact that even Jesus needed to learn to obey his father.

> [8]Son though he was, he learned
> obedience from what he suffered [9]and,
> once made perfect, he became the source
> of eternal salvation for all who obey
> him.
>
> *Hebrews 5:8-9*

....

God asks us to obey not because he desires the obedience in itself but because he's telling us how to play a game he designed. In the process of teaching us the game we get to know him better and trust him more which builds the very relationship that he desires. This furthers our reliance on him and lets us learn new things. That begins to put the scripture in John in perspective.

> "Those who accept my commandments and obey them are the ones who love me. And because they love me, my Father will love them. And I will love them and reveal myself to each of them."
>
> *John 14:21*

By playing the game with God we get to know him better. He reveals himself to us, not as some reward for the sacrifices made, but because we've spent time with the coach and begin to trust him. We run the plays and find out that is how the game is played and how to enjoy it more. It happens by default when we obey him.

Reflection: Let's take a minute and let this sink in. This concept is transformational if you can really internalize it. Thinking God wants me to obey his commandments or I'll have hell to pay has got to be let go. This line of thinking isn't even rational if you have believed and confessed that Jesus Christ is Lord. So why does it stick around lurking in the shadows of our minds?

Can you see the slight twist of truth the devil has played by keeping us stuck in trying to obtain salvation over and over through our actions? Stop trying to show God one grand gesture of repentance and start believing God knows how this game works and he has given you the secrets to playing it. Live obediently.

Do you believe God's way is the best way?

_____

_____

_____

How does your life reflect your belief, or does it?

_____

_____

_____

What are you going to do about it?

_____

_____

_____

CHAPTER 7:

POWER IN PEOPLE

LIFE IS NOT MEANT TO BE LIVED ALONE

Community....It's a buzzword pushed in most churches today. We hear pastor after pastor tell us we need to live in community. They say we are supposed to "do life" together. But was does that mean? It's odd that community is a concept so frequently mentioned, sometimes referenced as though it's critical, but rarely explained. What is it? How many people are there supposed to be in my community? Is my church my community? My small group? My bible study group? My friends? Does it mean leaving the world behind and living in a commune? Why does it matter? Does the bible even really mention community? As with most things it's hard to do something if you don't understand why you are called to do it. That is what we'll dive into in this chapter. What is biblical community and do we really need it?

THE BIBLE AND COMMUNITY

Our Creator is a communal God. As we discovered in chapter 2 he exists in three separate and distinct parts with unique purposes. Three existences of the same God. Now look at what the word has to say about us.

> "So God created human beings in his own image. In the image of God he created them; male and female he created them."
>
> *Genesis 1:27*

If we are made in his image then we too are creatures of community. "SEPARATELY IMPERFECT" if you will. When we reflect on this, it's pretty clear humans are hardwired for relationships, fellowship, and community. It is this very desire that the enemy manipulates to create havoc. The felling that you don't belong or someone being starved for attention is one of the more common reasons for addiction, suicide, joining gangs, etc. Have you ever felt like no one wanted you? That no one would miss you if you were gone? Feeling truly alone is one of the worst forms of depression. What would happen to us if we were not around people. It may sound nice for a while, and there is something to be said for unplugging spending time alone with God, but that is for a fleeting moment. Being isolated from other humans is torture even for the darkest of men. Just watch a documentary on solitary confinement. Inmates will often cut themselves and rub their blood all over the windows until no one can see through just to have an interaction with another person. Humans at their core need other humans to survive, to thrive, to experience happiness. We are going against our very creation, our DNA, when we choose to isolate and withdraw from others. We can clearly see the need for human interaction but what does the bible say about relationships? Let's start by looking at the creation of man. If you go back to the story of creation we see that God created all things in 6 days.

(A side note is warranted here. Many people have an issue with the creation story since science is clear that the world was not created in 6 days. We should consider what the definition of a day is....one rotation of the earth. How can you measure something by something that does not yet exist. The bible is clear that a "God day" is not the same thing as a revolution of the earth on its axis. Reference 2 Peter 3:8 & Psalms 90:4. Now back to the point)

Each time that God finished a creation he looked at it and saw that it was good" except when he created man.

> "Then the Lord God said, "it is not good for the man to be alone. I will make a helper who is just right for him."
>
> *Genesis 2:18*

That makes it pretty clear when the first thing that God sees as less than perfect is a being, created in his own image, that was alone. What else does scripture say about the necessity of community?

> "24And let us consider how we may spur one another on toward love and good deeds, 25not giving up meeting together, as some are in the habit of doing, but encouraging one another—and all the more as you see the Day approaching."
>
> *Hebrews 10:24-25*

"How good and pleasant it is when
God's people live together in unity!"

Psalm 133:1

....

"For where two or three gather in my
name, there am I with them."

Matthew 18:20

....

"For just as each of us has one body
with many members, and these members do
not all have the same function, so in
Christ we, though many, form one body, and
each member belongs to all the others."

Romans 12:4-5

....

"And over all these virtues put on
love, which binds them all together in
perfect unity."

Colossians 3:14

....

"For just as each of us has one body
with many members, and these members do
not all have the same function, so in
Christ we, though many, form one body, and
each member belongs to all the others."

Romans 12:4-5

....

"Live in harmony with one another. Do
not be proud, but be willing to associate
with people of low position. Do not be
conceited."

Romans 12:16

....

"All the believers were one in heart
and mind. No one claimed that any of
their possessions was their own, but they
shared everything they had."

Acts 4:32

....

"Make every effort to keep the unity
of the Spirit through the bond of peace."

Ephesians 4:3

....

Very truly I tell you, whoever accepts
anyone I send accepts me; and whoever
accepts me accepts the one who sent me.

John 13:20

....

And that's just the verses that are explicit! At this point it should be clear that God has built us for community and relationships but what does that really mean? What is community? For the answer to this we look to the life of Jesus. If he was really just a person, like you and I are then we should be able to see a picture of community in his life. Surprisingly enough we can. His life demonstrates three layers of community all of which are necessary for every christian to effectively follow God.

THE CAPITAL 'C' CHURCH

The Capital 'C' Church is the christian community as a whole. For Jesus it was the bulk followers of Christ. Remember when he fed the 5,000 or the 4,000? Or when he rode into Jerusalem on a donkey (Palm Sunday)? It was the masses of people that followed Christ to see his miracles and hear him speak. For us this is the whole body of believers of Christ. The Church is the primary evangelical source of spreading the news of Christ. This is where most nonbelievers will go when they begin to seek after God (though it is noteworthy they will usually go there because of a personal invite or relationship). For most of us this also includes the weekend services you might attend.

The Church serves as a place where we can come into community for worship and to be built up through sermons and teaching. This is the place where we get to use our gifts and talents inside the church to make it function at its best. We are able to impact people we would otherwise never meet with our service, tithe, and time. For Christians the church certainly builds and equips us but it does not exist for us. We, as the church, exist to show the world that it needs Christ. This is a massive oversimplification of the Capital 'C' Church but frankly it is one that we see demonstrated least in the bible. The leaders of the early church certainly met and made decisions for the church but most of the biblical descriptions of the church are really representations of the local church and not the Capital 'C' Church. That said, this level of community is vital to reaching the lost and building Christians to walk in their God called purpose.

Reflection:

Write your three top reasons for attending church.

_____

_____

_____

_____

_____

_____

Write three top reasons to not attend church.

_____

_____

_____

_____

_____

_____

YOUR LOCAL CHURCH

Did Jesus have a church? At first glance you would probably say yes, the sermon on the mount, meeting at the temple, feeding the 5000 or the 4000. But we showed that those were the capital 'C' church above, right? What was his local church? In short, his disciples and the women that traveled with him. Yes, the women were important too. So important that they were actually mentioned in a time where women were footnotes at best.

> "¹After this, Jesus traveled about from one town and village to another, proclaiming the good news of the kingdom of God. The Twelve were with him, ²and also some women who had been cured of evil spirits and diseases: Mary (called Magdalene) from whom seven demons had come out; ³Joanna the wife of Chuza, the manager of Herod's household; Susanna; and many others. These women were helping to support them out of their own means.
>
> *Luke 8:1*

If you need further proof read about the resurrection of Christ and note who were the first people to find out Jesus had risen. That wasn't an accident. The angel could have appeared to anybody at any time.

That brings us to the next point. How were these people different to Jesus than all the rest of his followers?

"¹⁰When he was alone, the Twelve and the others around him asked him about the parables. ¹¹He told them, "The secret of the kingdom of God has been given to you. But to those on the outside everything is said in parables ¹²so that, "they may be ever seeing but never perceiving, and ever hearing but never understanding; otherwise they might turn and be forgiven!"

Mark 4:10-12

....

He did not say anything to them without using a parable. But when he was alone with his own disciples, he explained everything.

Mark 4:34

....

Jesus took special time to build up and explain himself to his disciples. These would be the men (and women) that God would commission to go and start the church. They needed an extra depth of teaching. A deeper relationship with Jesus. They were his local church.

Before you check this level of community as met by going to church every weekend it's relevant that we look at what the early biblical church was.

"²And to our beloved Apphia, and Archippus our fellow soldier, and to the church in thy house:"

Philemon 1:2

....

"⁴⁶And they, continuing daily with one accord in the temple, and breaking bread from house to house, did eat their meat with gladness and singleness of heart,"

Acts 2:46

....

"¹⁹The churches in the province of Asia send you greetings. Aquila and Priscilla greet you warmly in the Lord, and so does the church that meets at their house."

1 Corinthians 16:19

....

"⁵Greet also the church that meets at their house. Greet my dear friend Epenetus, who was the first convert to Christ in the province of Asia."

Romans 16:5

....

Notice that in each instance it's a group of believers meeting in someone's home. This shows that it wasn't a massive group of hundreds of people coming together to learn God's word, that was what happened at the temple. This was a relatively small group of people that share things and do life together. In today's world of "Mega Churches" the term church has been a little distorted. Those churches are certainly part of the capital C church and they are doing an amazing job of furthering the gospel but they are not what was intended when the Bible talks about your "group of believers" or what we call your "local church". For those of us who attend a relatively small church this may truly be your local church but that is probably more of the exception than the rule for Christians today. So how do we tell the difference?

When you walk into the room where your church is meeting can you walk up to nearly every person in the room and know them by name? Do you know their spouse and how many kids they have? Do you know where they live? If not, that probably isn't your local church and you need to find a local church to plug into. It should probably be composed of a group of people from your weekly church service. You should get together regularly and study the bible, discuss God, and just hang out. Think more of a life group, bible study, home group, or house group than "Church".

It's at this level of community that the analogy of the forest and trees really becomes effective. The tallest tree on earth is Hyperion in the redwood forests of California. This tree stands 379' tall. That is taller than the Leaning Tower of Pisa, the Statue of Liberty and Big Ben in England.

The amazing thing is it's not really all that uncommon for redwood trees to grow several hundred feet tall.

When you see those massive trees it's natural to think that they have a massively deep root structure to support that kind of height. Surprisingly that is not the case in this giant and the other redwoods. The roots on these monster trees are only 3-5 feet deep. How is it possible that such an enormous tree can be supported by such a shallow root system? The secret of these trees is that the roots spread out, intertwine, connect, and even fuse with the roots of its neighbor. Creating a "single" super foundation that benefits the entire community of trees. Without the root system of each individual tree interlocking and sharing in the burdens of the forest they could never stand so tall. Every small tree shares in the success of the larger tree and vice-versa. Something like this is the system Paul envisioned in the book of Romans.

> "So in Christ we, though many, form one body, and each member belongs to all the others."
>
> *Romans 12:5*

Now read this scripture with this in mind.

> "For just as the body is one and has many members, and all the members of the body, though many, are one body, so it is with Christ. For in one Spirit we were all baptized into one body—Jews or Greeks, slaves or free—and all were made to drink of one Spirit. For the body

does not consist of one member but of
many. If the foot should say, "Because
I am not a hand, I do not belong to the
body," that would not make it any less a
part of the body. And if the ear should
say, "Because I am not an eye, I do not
belong to the body," that would not make
it any less a part of the body. If the
whole body were an eye, where would be
the sense of hearing? If the whole body
were an ear, where would be the sense of
smell?18 But as it is, God arranged the
members in the body, each one of them, as
he chose. If all were a single member,
where would the body be? As it is, there
are many parts, yet one body. The eye
cannot say to the hand, "I have no need
of you," nor again the head to the feet,
"I have no need of you." On the contrary,
the parts of the body that seem to be
weaker are indispensable, and on those
parts of the body that we think less
honorable we bestow the greater honor,
and our unpresentable parts are treated
with greater modesty, which our more
presentable parts do not require. But God
has so composed the body, giving greater
honor to the part that lacked it, that
there may be no division in the body, but
that the members may have the same care
for one another. If one member suffers,
all suffer together; if one member is
honored, all rejoice together.

1 Corinthians 12:12-26

This is a perfect picture of the local church, "That there may be no division in the body." All too often people leave their "church" with the thought that they don't fit in, they don't have a sense of belonging. They are outclassed, under appreciated, not noticed, taken advantage of, or insulted. The reality is we need to be different. Like Paul says if the eye says to the hand I don't need you it is only fooling itself. If we were all ears the body would be lacking.

So the next time you feel like you don't belong, take it as an indication that you are exactly what that "body" of people need. We are quick to find like people to be around but the true beauty of humanity is the fact that we are all different. We should be looking for people that challenge the way we think and live our lives so that we may mature in the ways of God and balance out each others faults. If everyone around you is bad at the same things you are will improving those things ever be accomplished in your life? If you are taking advice about your marriage from someone that has been divorced three times already how good do you think that advice is? It's certainly not worthless but it is probably lacking some perspective.

We need a community of diverse people to lean on so that their roots (background, struggles, strengths, and weaknesses) become a part of the root structure of our life. This will help you overcome all the strategies of the enemy who is trying to steal, kill, and destroy you and everything you love. Doing this in the local church not only gives you an army to hold you up but a battalion of soldiers to pray for you as well. If you think you are not wanted or under appreciated consider your lungs or your kidneys. The things you don't really notice until there is a problem but without them you would die. Same with the people in your church that just keep doing what they do every day.

The truly amazing thing about a community of trees is what they do to the environment around them. Think about it, when you approach a forest of trees it becomes the dominant portion of the landscape. It is the trees that define the environment you live in. It is the same way with an effective community of believers. As they grow and strengthen each other they redefine their environment. They start becoming the dominant portion of the landscape. The place they live begins to look different. They change the ecosystem.

Not only do they support each other but they also form a canopy of leaves. This canopy forms a protective covering that protects the undergrowth when storms, heavy rains, and hail come. It traps in moisture and protects the plants from the sun's scorching rays. Think about that the next time you want to leave a church because someone hurt your feelings. When you leave now there is a hole that the storm can rain down on the sprouts and kill them out. When someone withdraws from a community it leaves it vulnerable to attack. Thoughts creep into the minds of your friends and acquaintances that maybe they are not in the right place. A sprouting tree with little to no roots may see this and fall away completely. When we stay united as "one" we can bring care, protection, healing, and encouragement to so many more people than we ever could alone.

So that proves the necessity for this level of community but what should we be doing in our community? In today's world people get overwhelmed with social media and making "Friends" but as a whole we have never been further away from true relationships. We talk (text) and see (videos) each other through a filter that is controllable. Leaving out all the surprises, all the nuances, and ultimately allowing people to project an image that could not be further from the truth. Not many people are truly vulnerable, transparent, and genuine. As a result many people struggle with the fundamental question. Who am I? We spend so much time being who we want to be or who we think others want us to be that we never truly be ourselves. We may know what our friends are doing, where they are, or even what there eating for dinner but we have no idea who they really are. We get plastic people living in a fake world desperately reaching for something real. Something to numb the void and emptiness of broken promises that our devices and filtered relationships give us.

The local church is the solution to this. A place to be transparent and real. A place to take your needs and gifts. A place to belong and be known. This should be your best friends and closest relationships. If done correctly it's amazing what the church can do.

"³³With great power the apostles
continued to testify to the resurrection
of the Lord Jesus. And God's grace was
so powerfully at work in them all 34that
there were no needy persons among them.
For from time to time those who owned
land or houses sold them, brought the
money from the sales ³⁵and put it at the
apostles' feet, and it was distributed to
anyone who had need."

Acts 4:33

There was no needy among them. The church takes care of itself. When there is a need it meets it. They know each other and pray for them.

This is the most transformational and meaningful part of the christian community. When we do this correctly people begin to see it and they naturally want it. They are drawn to it. We are built to have community and it is this level of community that meets that inherent need. The bible demonstrates this very principle.

"⁴⁴All the believers were together and had everything in common. 45They sold property and possessions to give to anyone who had need. ⁴⁶Every day they continued to meet together in the temple courts. They broke bread in their homes and ate together with glad and sincere hearts, ⁴⁷praising God and enjoying the favor of all the people. And the Lord added to their number daily those who were being saved."

Acts 2:44-47

When we gather as a church we become something bigger than ourselves. We change the spiritual ecosystem around us. We protect those within the community creating a safe place for hurting people to come and feel important and loved. We get to see new believers come to God for the first time over and over again as the number of God's army increases day by day. We get a unique opportunity to pray for the real needs of the real people around us. As we see God meet the needs of those around us it waters our tree. We see his faithfulness at work and our faith gets stronger. We live the struggles of those around us and sometimes get to be a part of God answering prayer. We grow "taller" and closer to God then we could ever do on our own. In all of this one underlying theme stays consistent. Our faith is strengthened!!

YOUR BROTHERS/SISTERS

The final level of christian community is that of a close personal relationship with a very small group of people. This group cannot effectively be more than five people but should not be less than two (in addition to yourself). Jesus demonstrated this level of community with three disciples, Peter, James, and John. The bible records three times that Jesus took only these three men with Him. When he raised the Daughter of Jairus from the dead.

> "[37]He did not let anyone follow him except Peter, James and John the brother of James. [38]When they came to the home of the synagogue leader, Jesus saw a commotion, with people crying and wailing loudly. [39]He went in and said to them, "Why all this commotion and wailing? The child is not dead but asleep."[40]But they laughed at him."
>
> *Mark 5:37-40*

When he was transformed at the mount of Transfiguration.

"¹After six days Jesus took with him Peter, James and John the brother of James, and led them up a high mountain by themselves. ²There he was transfigured before them. His face shone like the sun, and his clothes became as white as the light. 3Just then there appeared before them Moses and Elijah, talking with Jesus."

Matthew 17:1-3

And to the Garden of Gethsemane.

"³²They went to a place called Gethsemane, and Jesus said to his disciples, "Sit here while I pray."³³He took Peter, James and John along with him, and he began to be deeply distressed and troubled. ³⁴"My soul is overwhelmed with sorrow to the point of death,"he said to them. "Stay here and keep watch."

Mark 14:32-34

These men were Jesus' close personal friends whom he showed his most intimate and true parts of his being. Think about it, they were literally shown the glory of Christ on the mount of transfiguration. Not only that but they got to hear the true voice of God himself.

> ⁷Then a cloud appeared and covered
> them, and a voice came from the cloud:
> "This is my Son, whom I love. Listen to
> him!"

Mark 9:7

....

The way Jesus demonstrated the need for this level of community starts to put the words of Solomon in better perspective.

> "Two people are better off than one,
> for they can help each other succeed. If
> one person falls, the other can reach out
> and help. But someone who falls alone is
> in real trouble. Likewise, two people
> lying close together can keep each other
> warm. But how can one be warm alone? A
> person standing alone can be attacked
> and defeated, but two can stand back-to-
> back and conquer. Three are even better,
> for a triple-braided cord is not easily
> broken."

Ecclesiastes 4: 9-12

....

That is pretty clear. A man alone is at risk and dangerous. But there is a more subtle point that is easily overlooked. If you are not there to stand back-to-back with your close brother they "can be attacked and defeated." This is incredibly important, it's not all about you. It's about how you can build those God has put in your life.

Look back at when Jesus took just the three with him.

When he was going to raise a girl from the dead, what does it say the people did before he acted? They laughed at him. Why did he take them with him to the Garden? Because he was going to do something hard.

Think about it, Jesus had to say and do some pretty wild things in the course of his ministry and when he had to do the most challenging of them he took his best friends. Someone who had his back and supported him unequivocally. He was human and needed his friends for support. Jesus needed them. Without embracing this perspective it is impossible to apply this level of christian community effectively. Jesus, the divinely empowered son of God, needed other men to complete his mission. How can we possibly hope to do what we are called to do without the very same thing?

So what does that look like for us today? That answer is complicated and a little painful but can be summarized as Faith, Honesty, and Humility.

Let's be honest, you don't want to go to church or a small group and explain to everyone that you got wasted three times last week, looked at porn, and lost your temper. This is where the one on one intimate relationships become critical. Have you ever had someone in your life you can say anything to without fear of being judged or ridiculed for your actions or thoughts? Someone that will listen to you vent without needing to critique your thought process or tell you where you went wrong? If not, it is imperative to cultivate this kind of relationship with another person of the same sex. You can be transparent with your spouse and that's great but you need someone outside of that relationship to help you filter through issues you can't bring up with your spouse (at least not at that moment).

When you expose the dark places of your life to your trusted friends it allows the door to be opened for Christ to come in and shine the light. He says "For where two or three gather together as my followers, I am there among them." This is really important. When you begin to seek God and discuss your most intimate issues with a close friend, Christ is among you. Think about what scripture tells us Christ did everywhere he went. The lame walked, the blind see, what was dead came to life, and time after time he forgave sins. To be in a deep, personal, vulnerable relationship takes faith and sacrifice. It takes faith that the person you are confessing to and confiding in will not use the information against you or make you feel worse than you already do. Faith that the person will be there for you just as you are there for them. Faith they will not abuse the trust and the relationship. It takes sacrifice of life's most precious commodity, time. We have seen how God has chosen to limit his power on earth to working through men in the channel of faith so when we are in a relationship that requires faith it opens the channel for Christ to work hence the scripture "For where two or three gather together as my followers, I am there among them." Please let this sink in. An intimate relationship allows Christ to work through another person, on your heart and in doing so grow your faith, forgive your sins, and healing your wounds.

The channel of faith can't work unless we are willing to humble ourselves and be truly honest about our thoughts and fears. When you humble yourself and take on a posture of vulnerability you expose your darkest parts to the light then Christ is then able to remove these things and bring healing and renewal. It is hard to do. Terrifying at times but is there truly any faith without fear or risk? This will not happen if you do not talk about it. You think you can handle it on your own? How has that been working out for you? That same old crap is still haunting you. Telling you not to tell anyone because they won't understand. They will never look at you the same. They will never forgive you. You're terrified of it. But remember:

> `"⁷For God has not given us a spirit of`
> `fear and timidity, but of power, love,`
> `and self-discipline."`
>
> *2 Timothy 1:7*

Fear is of the enemy. We must turn around confront the fear and dig in with our friends. To be honest at times but the fear never goes away. There is an old analogy that represents this perfectly. Let's say you have some leftovers that you put in a container and left in your fridge. You don't get around to eating it and it begins to mold. You see it in the back of the fridge but it grosses you out touch it so you just leave it there. Maybe you're just lazy and don't like to clean. For whatever reason you just ignore it and let it sit there. It gets so bad that it makes your entire fridge, and everything in it, begin to smell. Now the thing you are refusing to deal with, to get out and clean, is now contaminating every good thing you put in your fridge. Until you put on your big boy pants, grab ahold of the nasty stinky container and get rid of it, every good thing you put in will come out smelling like rot.

The bible confirms this.

> "Confess your sins to each other and pray for each other so that you may be healed. The earnest prayer of a righteous person has great power and produces wonderful results."
>
> *James 5:16*

So the transparency of a close personal relationship creates the environment for God to work but that is not all this scripture says. It says that it is the prayers of that person that produce wonderful results. You can do it alone. You need to confess and ask for help. HUMILITY.

> "The greatest among you must be a servant. But those who exalt themselves will be humbled, and those who humble themselves will be exalted."
>
> *Matthew 23:11-12*

When we take our problems and needs to our close friends they come alongside us in action and prayer.

They see a need and they meet that need. They go storming into the throne room of our heavenly father begging for his help with the situation. They do the knee work. When you do it right you start finding yourself needing their input and advice before you make a decision. You can predict what their reaction to something is better than their spouse and they can do the same for you. They are brothers in arms ready to do war for not just you but all those around you. Your spouse, your kids, your parents, your boss, and that complete stranger that God put on your heart. When something goes wrong with you or inside your family, your whole family knows they can go to your brother/sister for help. You don't have to worry about straying from God's path because they are walking that same path and you can't imagine walking without them. When you make a stupid decision they tell you your an idiot then bend down, pick you up, and give you a hug. They then put you on their shoulders and carry you back to the path. The Bible is so clear about this.

> `"`¹⁷`A friend loves at all times, and a`
> `brother is born for a time of adversity.`
>
> *Proverbs 17:17*

It's a beautiful picture that we all really desire but our pride, dishonesty, and fear keep us from it. The pretty picture is great but the opposite is even more terrifying. When you don't have a brother in arms you find yourself vulnerable. No one feeds you, challenges you, or motivates you. You do some things for God but without the faith of your friends you'll find your impact small and limited. That's the best case, but for many, it's far more dire. You fight with your spouse and decide to go hangout at the bar to drown your sorrows. You make a bad decision and now your situation is worse than when you started. Your kids start hanging out with the wrong crowd and won't listen to you. They've got no one else to speak into them and just plow down that path. You have a moment of weakness and turn back to your old habits. No one is close to you to see the misstep so you just keep going. It spirals out of control taking your whole life. Solomon said this so well.

> "⁹Two are better than one, because they have a good return for their labor: ¹⁰If either of them falls down, one can help the other up. But pity anyone who falls and has no one to help them up. ¹¹Also, if two lie down together, they will keep warm. But how can one keep warm alone? ¹²Though one may be overpowered, two can defend themselves. A cord of three strands is not quickly broken."
>
> *Ecclesiastes 4:9-12*

Reflection: Think about a time when you finally broke down and confessed a sin that you had been holding on to, ignoring, or compartmentalizing. Who was it? Why did you confess? How did you feel before? How did you feel after?

_____

_____

_____

_____

_____

Now write the main reason you are still holding onto your sins instead of following James advice.

_____

_____

_____

_____

_____

Action: If you do not have a close transparent relationship with another christian (of the same sex) make a plan to create or develop one from a current friendship.

CHAPTER 8:

WHEN GOD DOESN'T CARE?

WHAT TO DO WHEN GOD DOESN'T LISTEN.

Reflection: Think back on your life... how many different ways have you been instructed to pray? How many ways have you tried? (By yourself, with others, out loud, in your head, on your knees, in tongues, etc). Does one way seem more effective than others? Did the confusion of it all frustrate you? Have you ever felt like you couldn't quite figure it out and that's why your prayers aren't answered?

_____

_____

_____

_____

_____

_____

_____

_____

_____

_____

_____

_____

If we are going to discuss prayer then we should probably address the elephant in the room. What happens when we pray for something, really believe god will answer it and nothing happens? Many of us get concerned that we didn't do it right. Let's be honest if God is slow to answer, or if the answer is no, many of us believe that confirms our prayer was flawed or just plain inept. Perhaps we believe that we are not good enough to have our prayers answered. We haven't earned it. We don't deserve it. Maybe even deeper than that; Maybe God just doesn't care enough to answer. There are many scriptures that certainly appear to confirm this view of unanswered prayers. Jesus himself said.

> [24]Therefore I tell you, whatever you ask for in prayer, believe that you have received it, and it will be yours.
>
> *Mark 11: 24*

That seems pretty clear. If we want something, believe we will get it, and pray for it then we get it. It's further confirmed in the scripture preceding verse 24.

> [22] "Have faith in God," Jesus answered. [23]"Truly I tell you, if anyone says to this mountain, 'Go, throw yourself into the sea,' and does not doubt in their heart but believes that what they say will happen, it will be done for them.
>
> *Mark 11:22-23*

Straightforward and simple. If we pray for something and don't get it then it's obviously because we lacked the faith.

> *Reflection: How do you process your unanswered prayers? Do you believe you didn't pray right and start calculating the correct way to approach God with your request? Do you believe since you sinned earlier God is punishing you by not listening and/or acting? Do you precede your prayers asking for forgiveness of your sins in hopes that he will hear you this time? Do you feel like God doesn't care? How do you classify your unanswered prayers?*

_____

_____

_____

_____

_____

_____

_____

_____

_____

_____

RECAP: Straightforward and simple. If we pray for something and don't get it then it's obviously because we lacked the faith, right??

The problem with this logic is that it is based in our understanding and in the world's view of logic itself. God's economy doesn't function based on the world's system of cause and effect. Think of the many counterintuitive statements in the bible. Those who lose their life will find it but those who find their life will lose it. It is by grace you have been saved, not of works. He who humbles himself will be exalted but he who exalts himself shall be humbled. We need to remember that God exists outside of the restraints of time so cause and effect happen simultaneously. Time and time again God demonstrates that he is playing a different game than we are and his game is always the long game. Wordly or human logic works fine if you're playing checkers but the spiritual realm is really a game of chess. We must always remember:

> 8"For my thoughts are not your thoughts, neither are your ways my ways," declares the Lord. 9"As the heavens are higher than the earth, so are my ways higher than your ways and my thoughts than your thoughts.
>
> *Isaiah 55:8-9*

We serve a God that experiences yesterday, today, and tomorrow all at the same time, therefore, cause and effect have a vastly different meaning. When we begin applying our understanding to his processes we will often be left confused and broken. He is a being of unfathomable power, grace, and mercy. We simply don't have his capacity to determine what is good and what is bad because we can't see the endgame. Situations are even further complicated by Romans 8:28.

> ²⁸ And we know that in all things God works for the good of those who love him, who have been called according to his purpose.
>
> Romans 8:28

Even the things that are bad will work for our good. The bible gives us a story of a man who got the opportunity to question God. It's the story of Job. The CliffsNotes version of this story is that the devil bet God that he could make Job curse his name.

The bible describes Job as a "blameless and upright" man, so much so that God prompted Satan to consider him for their bet. With God removing his protection from Job, the devil proceeds to take everything Job owns, kill all his children, and strike him with boils. Job's friends then come by and spend several chapters arguing with Job and explaining to him various reasons why he must deserve the things that happened to him. After all "God is Just" they say. They prepare some very compelling arguments but none that Job agrees with because he knows he has been blameless before God.

In the end, Job refuses to curse God. Even when asked to do so by his own wife, and is afforded a very, very rare opportunity. God himself confronts Job and responds to his questions. "What did God say?

> ¹Then the Lord spoke to Job out of the storm. He said: ²"Who is this that obscures my plans with words without knowledge? ³Brace yourself like a man; I will question you, and you shall answer me.
>
> *Job 38:1-3*

He then proceeds to spend four chapters asking Job to explain how various things in nature work and asking Job if he can do things like tame a leviathan. After four chapters of withering reproach from God this is what Job had to say.

> ¹Then Job replied to the Lord: ²"I know that you can do all things; no purpose of yours can be thwarted. ³You asked, 'Who is this that obscures my plans without knowledge?' Surely I spoke of things I did not understand, things too wonderful for me to know. ⁴"You said, ''Listen now, and I will speak; I will question you, and you shall answer me.' ⁵My ears had heard of you but now my eyes have seen you. ⁶Therefore I despise myself and repent in dust and ashes."
>
> *Job 42: 1-6*

That is an incredibly telling statement about God. From nearly any perspective there is no person in the bible that had more of a right to question, and/or be angry with God than Job. He was upstanding and blameless before God yet he lost everything in order for God to win a contest with Satan. He had every right, using worldly logic, to demand answers from God, and demand some sort of explanation. All that righteous entitlement and when God presents himself to Job to answer his question all Job can do is say I thought I understood you but I had no idea. I'm sorry. Please accept my deepest and most sincere apologies. The lesson to take from this is simple. **Don't expect to understand God and how he works**. We are too simple and too slow. When we get the smallest glimpse of his might and majesty all we can do is apologize and look away. This is another example of us returning to the original sin in the garden.

"I can be as God, knowing good from evil."

So, with that upbeat and positive outlook on how we should view the idea of understanding God's plan and his answers, or lack thereof, you might be thinking there is little purpose to the discussion of unanswered prayers. If the answer is we may never know, and really shouldn't expect to know, then why should we discuss them at all? Simply put, embracing the concept that God's ways are truly higher than our ways allows us the freedom to change our question. It allows us to stop testing God with a "Why" question that likely has an answer we can't understand. Instead we can focus our thoughts and efforts on what we should **DO** when we think God isn't answering our prayers. When we think God isn't answering our prayers we should follow a three step process.

#1 - DON'T ASSUME WE UNDERSTAND WHY OR WHAT GOD IS DOING.

When we pray and we don't see God acting we shouldn't start making assumptions about what God's doing or not doing. One author put this very succinctly as "resist the urge to connect the dots". As a human it's easy to see a cause and effect or a series of events and assume we understand why it happened and start projecting that understanding into what will happen next. We prayed and nothing happened therefore God isn't going to answer that prayer. We prayed and nothing happened so we must have done it wrong or not be worthy. We prayed and nothing happened so God must not care. One dot must connect to the next. We must always remember:

Just because we don't see something happening doesn't mean God isn't doing something.

How quickly do you expect god to act when you pray? If you pray for healing are you expecting immediate relief? If you pray that you and your spouse stop fighting and get along, do you expect the issues to just disappear? If you pray for your kids to stop making horrible decisions, do you expect for God to turn them around on a dime? Maybe we don't see God working because our perspective is in line with this microwave mentality world. Yes God can and does provide immediate results for prayers, but not very often. If God gave us immediate results for all of our prayers how would that grow your faith tree. If you gave a toddler everything they asked for anytime they asked for it, they would probably be dead or injured within a week. Everything grows stronger under tension and resistance, our relationship with God is no different. Faith isn't belief backed by hard evidence but belief even when there appears to be a lack thereof.

```
    For in hope we have been saved, but
hope that is seen is not hope; for who
hopes for what he already sees?
```

Romans 8:24

....

```
    Now faith is the assurance of things
hoped for, the conviction of things not
seen.
```

Hebrews 1:11

....

It doesn't mean we are not worthy.

Several of us think we don't get what we pray for because we are not good enough or God doesn't care because I did _____. Sounds like Job's friends from the story above. You get what you deserve...you made your bed.....you haven't earned it....right? Is that how you obtained your salvation? Grace is the exact opposite of this way of thinking. You are worth God sending his son to suffer and die at the hands of men simply to open the door for you to be reunited with him. If that's the case then you are more than worthy of being heard by that same God.

> ⁹But you are a chosen people, a royal
> priesthood, a holy nation, God's special
> possession, that you may declare the
> praises of him who called you out of
> darkness into his wonderful light.
>
> *1 Peter 2:9*

It certainly doesn't mean we should question the goodness of God.

God does not enjoy punishing us. It breaks his heart to see his children addicted, hateful, abusive, suicidal, etc. He may not cause it and he certainly doesn't like it but he will always use it. We have all felt like God is punishing us in the hard times. The truth is most of the time we either caused the trouble ourselves or another lost and confused person caused it.

It's all part of the amazing gift of free will. However the Father who loves us so much uses the pain for a purpose.

> ⁹The Lord is good to all; he has
> compassion on all he has made.
>
> *Psalm 145:9*

We've already gone over it above but it's worth stating again. God is bigger than us and his plans are way beyond our understanding. Human logic doesn't apply to Godly plans. Understanding the plans and processes of God can be compared to doing an old school Dot-to-Dot puzzle. You might remember these from when you were a kid as a picture with a series of dots with numbers beside them. Pretty simple process right? We often look at God's plan as just a series of dots that need to be connected to reveal the final picture that demonstrates what it's all about. The problem with us connecting the dots is that we don't understand God's numbering system. For us it's just some funny symbols next to the dots. The picture is just a bunch of dots to connect and the only way we know which dot comes next is because we ASSUME we know what the final picture is supposed to look like. We start connecting the dots using human "logic" and then are surprised the picture we come up with is wrong. We are playing dot to dot but we don't know how to count!

Before you walk away from this thinking God is an impartial butt hole that just doesn't want to explain things. I think it's important to remember our position relative to God. He is our heavenly Father and as such sees things differently. The problem many people have with this analogy is they relate it to their current or most recent relationship with their father i.e. as an adult to another more learned adult. That isn't the proper perspective. The father relationship is that of a father with a toddler. Think about it. When your father explained something complicated to you, or you explain something to your young child, did you go into great detail about it or the hard realities around it? How would you tackle a difficult question from a 3 or 4 year old?

What if they asked you about taxes? Would you explain to them the detailed purposes of taxes and exactly how they are calculated (as if you really know.....) or would you give a "50,000 foot" answer that gives the general idea and leaves out the details? Will they be able to understand the math or concepts? How about a question about drug use and addiction? Divorce? Death? Lust? Pornography? Would you delve into the dirty details? Would you explain all the different reasons things can go wrong. Would doing so rob them of some of their innocence? Would it scare them and cause more damage than benefit?

This is how God sees our questions. We wonder why he won't explain it and the truth is we don't have the capacity to understand it. If we do, it will probably be more damaging than beneficial. He looks at us as a loving father looks at their toddler or preschooler and gives us the best answer we are capable of comprehending. He tries to guide us but has to do so through statements our simple minds can understand. Hence Christ only speaking in parables. Thinking of the relationship puts Jesus' words in a different perspective.

> "17Truly I tell you, anyone who will not receive the kingdom of God like a little child will never enter it."
>
> *Luke 18:17*

Reflection: Have you kept God in the proper perspective while praying? Do you really believe he knows what you need more than you do or do you get angry when the answers and/or results don't come?

_____

_____

_____

_____

_____

_____

_____

_____

_____

_____

_____

_____

_____

_____

#2 - ANALYZE OUR REQUEST AND OUR MOTIVATION FOR IT.

> ³When you ask, you do not receive, because you ask with wrong motives, that you may spend what you get on your pleasures.
>
> *James 4:3*

....

This is pretty simple, though it may be hard to admit and at times hard to see. If we are praying for something with the wrong motives it can cause those prayers to go unanswered. There are many ways that we cloud our motives and confuse our true intent. We may sugar coat the selfish motives with a rationalization; "If you give me that raise I'll be able to give more to the church/charity." Sometimes we approach it with an attitude of entitlement; "I've been reading my bible daily so you should answer this prayer request for healing." The good news is that there is a simple test that will evaluate the motives of your prayer. Ask yourself if you can honestly make this statement:

"If it isn't your will that this happen then I trust you and I'm ok with that. I want what you want for me more than what I want for me".

If you can't honestly say that, then your motives are corrupt. Even if it is something that is in God's will, at this point, you've made it an idol and it has become something that is separating you from God. In order to pray the most powerful and impassioned prayers you must subordinate your desires to God's will. Jesus demonstrated this very principle in the Garden of Gethsemane.

> [42]"Father, if you are willing, take
> this cup from me; yet not my will, but
> yours be done."

Luke 22:42

....

There is no better example of praying with the correct motives. When confronted with his own suffering and death, Jesus went to his father and begged him not to do it. He asked, please don't make this happen. Please do not make me go through this. I don't want to do it. Then, in the very same breath, he said but if it's what you want then I'll do it. "Yet not my will, but yours be done".....I want what you want more than what I want.

It's been said that God will be everything you need when God becomes everything you need. That puts your approach to God and his ability to answer prayer in a completely different light. When we realize God is everything that we need and his will for us represents the pinnacle of what we can accomplish than we can approach God with an unshakable faith. In that faith God provides everything that we need regardless of whether it's what we want. His good is always better than our great. In order for our motives to be correct we must always place the will of God above our desires.

Reflection: We are all born selfish. It happens so early in life. All you have to do is be around a two year old for 30 minutes and you will hear it...MINE!!!! Can you honestly say you want what God wants more than what you want?

_____

_____

_____

_____

_____

_____

_____

_____

_____

_____

_____

_____

_____

#3 - JUST KEEP PRAYING.

Once you've made sure you aren't making assumptions
about God's will and after you've tested your motives you
can proceed to this final step. If your motives are pure
and God hasn't answered that prayer, you just keep
praying. Apparently, a single ask is not always enough to
get something moving for God. The bible doesn't explicitly
tell us why this is but it does give us an instance where
persistent prayer was required. Daniel had been given a
message concerning a great war from God but he didn't
understand it. He asked God for understanding but
didn't get it. He began fasting and praying to God and
continued for 21 days (this is where we get the Daniel fast)
Finally this happened.

> [4]On the twenty-fourth day of the first
> month, as I was standing on the bank of
> the great river, the Tigris, [5]I looked up
> and there before me was a man dressed in
> linen, with a belt of fine gold from Uphaz
> around his waist. [6]His body was like
> topaz, his face like lightning, his eyes
> like flaming torches, his arms and legs
> like the gleam of burnished bronze, and
> his voice like the sound of a multitude.
>
> [7]I, Daniel, was the only one who saw
> the vision; those who were with me did
> not see it, but such terror overwhelmed
> them that they fled and hid themselves.
> [8]So I was left alone, gazing at this
> great vision; I had no strength left,
> my face turned deathly pale and I was
> helpless. [9]Then I heard him speaking, and

as I listened to him, I fell into a deep
sleep, my face to the ground.

¹⁰A hand touched me and set me trembling
on my hands and knees. ¹¹He said, "Daniel,
you who are highly esteemed, consider
carefully the words I am about to speak
to you, and stand up, for I have now been
sent to you." And when he said this to
me, I stood up trembling.

¹²Then he continued, "Do not be afraid,
Daniel. Since the first day that you set
your mind to gain understanding and to
humble yourself before your God, your
words were heard, and I have come in
response to them. ¹³But the prince of
the Persian kingdom resisted me twenty-
one days. Then Michael, one of the chief
princes, came to help me, because I was
detained there with the king of Persia.
¹⁴Now I have come to explain to you what
will happen to your people in the future,
for the vision concerns a time yet to
come."

Daniel 10:4-12

....

In this case, God dispatched an angel to answer Daniels
prayers the moment he started asking but that angel was
detained. Daniel kept praying and that eventually built up
enough steam to get God to dispatch the commander of
God's armies just to get Daniel's answer to him.

This directly relates to point number one, sometimes
things are happening but we just don't see them. Maybe
your request just needs a little more time, and a little

more prayer, so God can dispatch his armies to counter the enemy. The takeaway here should be that there are some things that require a more nagging approach of God. There are a couple of parables Jesus told about this very principle.

THE PARABLE OF THE FRIEND AT NIGHT

> Then Jesus said to them, "Suppose you have a friend, and you go to him at midnight and say, 'Friend, lend me three loaves of bread; a friend of mine on a journey has come to me, and I have no food to offer him.'And suppose the one inside answers, Don't bother me. The door is already locked, and my children and I are in bed. I can't get up and give you anything.'I tell you, even though he will not get up and give you the bread because of friendship, yet because of your shameless audacity he will surely get up and give you as much as you need.
>
> *Luke 11:5-8*

This parable is particularly interesting because it immediately follows the Lord's Prayer in Luke. When his disciples asked Jesus to teach them to pray he told them the Lord's Prayer then immediately told them this parable. The principle of persistent prayer must be incredibly important if that is the first thing Jesus follows a prayer demonstration with after being asked how to pray.

THE PARABLE OF THE PERSISTENT WIDOW

¹Then Jesus told his disciples a parable to show them that they should always pray and not give up. ²He said: "In a certain town there was a judge who neither feared God nor cared what people thought. ³And there was a widow in that town who kept coming to him with the plea, Grant me justice against my adversary.'

⁴"For some time he refused. But finally he said to himself, 'Even though I don't fear God or care what people think, ⁵yet because this widow keeps bothering me, I will see that she gets justice, so that she won't eventually come and attack me!' "

⁶And the Lord said, "Listen to what the unjust judge says. ⁷And will not God bring about justice for his chosen ones, who cry out to him day and night? Will he keep putting them off? ⁸I tell you, he will see that they get justice, and quickly. However, when the Son of Man comes, will he find faith on the earth?"

Luke 18:1-8

Again, Jesus clearly demonstrates the persistent prayer, even in the face of opposition, moves the heart of God. Perhaps this is the truest demonstration of faith. The war of attrition. The will to keep going back and asking because you know that God is good and he loves you. It's not unshakable faith that what you want will happen, it's the unshakable faith that God is good and he answers prayers. The relentless pursuit of him. Maybe this is what Jesus meant when he said if we have the faith to ask a mountain to move it will. Maybe it doesn't need to be a miraculous earthquake that moves the mountain, maybe it needs to be a long consistent rain that eventually erodes the mountain away.

The Best example of this is the last night of Jesus in the garden of Gethsemane. We read a short excerpt of the story of Gethsemane above but lets review the full account from Matthew.

> [36]Then Jesus went with his disciples to a place called Gethsemane, and he said to them, "Sit here while I go over there and pray."[37]He took Peter and the two sons of Zebedee along with him, and he began to be sorrowful and troubled. [38]Then he said to them, My soul is overwhelmed with sorrow to the point of death. Stay here and keep watch with me."

> [39]Going a little farther, he fell with his face to the ground and prayed, "My Father, if it is possible, may this cup be taken from me. Yet not as I will, but as you will."

> [40]Then he returned to his disciples and found them sleeping. "Couldn't you men keep watch with me for one hour?"he asked Peter. [41]"Watch and pray so that you will not fall into temptation. The spirit is willing, but the flesh is weak."

> [42]He went away a second time and prayed, "My Father, if it is not possible for this cup to be taken away unless I drink it, may your will be done."

> ⁴³When he came back, he again found
> them sleeping, because their eyes were
> heavy. ⁴⁴So he left them and went away
> once more and prayed the third time,
> saying the same thing.
>
> *Matthew 26:36-43*

Not once, not twice, but three times he is recorded as asking God to not make him go to the cross. This is just the times that are recorded at the very end. Do you think Jesus was just ignoring this in his prayer time prior to the garden? Surely not! When you are really dreading something that is going to happen in the near term future do you only think about it in the moment before it happens? I would wager that Jesus spent many hours talking with God about this and asking him to come up with another path. Jesus demonstrated the principle of asking for something we want even when God doesn't appear to be answering prayers. This should give us an amazing amount of confidence in approaching God and asking for what we want. There are not selfish prayers as long as you can still say, "I want what you want more".

An important note about Jesus' trip to the Garden of Gethsemane is that there is an account of it in all four Gospels. We've said it before but it bears repeating, something showing up in all four gospels is very rare and therefore must be critically important. Perhaps the importance of this is to demonstrate that Jesus's instructions about continuing to ask for something even when you don't see the results was more than just instruction for us. We often see parables and think they don't really apply to Jesus.

He is God on earth so his words weren't really applicable to him. Gethsemane proves that, at least in this case, it was his personal method of approaching his father. It was instruction on what we should do when it appears God is not answering our prayers. He demonstrated all three principles in one simple action. I would argue that Jesus was relatively certain at this point that God wasn't going to answer the prayer but he still kept asking. The takeaway?

Assume that your prayers are moving the heart of God until God moves yours.

When we continue to bring the same thing back to God in prayer over and over again it may begin to feel futile. But this is exactly what Jesus was doing and through that process God was moving his heart. In his first prayer he said. "My Father, if it is possible, may this cup be taken from me. Yet not as I will, but as you will." Then when he returned the second time. "My Father, if it is not possible for this cup to be taken away unless I drink it, may your will be done." Do you see the subtle difference? Jesus was trying to move God's heart but in the process God began to change his. Ultimately Jesus did not get what he was asking for but he did get an answer from heaven.

```
An angel from heaven appeared to him
and strengthened him.
```

Luke 22:43 NIV

Jesus got what he needed, strength for the trial to come, not what he asked for, the trial to pass.

"My grace is sufficient for you, for my
power is made perfect in weakness."

2 Corinthians 12:9

Let's put this in a different light. Was there ever a man that had more of a "right" to request something from God then Jesus? He had already given up a place in heaven to become fully human and live a tempted existence. He lived a perfect existence and never sinned. Was there anyone that understood how to pray for something better than Jesus? Surely he knew the correct technique to get God's ear. His request was totally reasonable, right? "I just don't want to be beaten, tortured and ultimately separated from you." What was the Garden of Gethsemane really? It was the greatest unanswered prayer. Never was there a more righteous and reasonable prayer, prayed by a more deserving man. Yet, what would have happened if God said "Ok nevermind Jesus"? God failing to answer Jesus' prayer is what covered your sins and allowed you to be reunited with God through the Holy Spirit. It paid our price and bridged the gap between man and God. Christianity was born from an unanswered prayer!

So what do we do?

1.   We don't assume we know what God is doing.

2.   We check our motives.

3.   We just keep praying.

Always assume that your prayers are moving the heart of God until God moves yours.

Reflection: What have you given up praying for? Why did you stop?

_____

_____

_____

_____

_____

_____

_____

_____

_____

_____

_____

_____

_____

_____

_____

_____

CHAPTER 9:

THE HEART
OF GOD

WE ARE RESPONSIBLE FOR
BREAKING GOD'S HEART

When we set out to write this book we truly believed the point was that we were made to be prayer warriors. Conduits of God's power on earth. Heavenly ambassador's to a fallen world. As we progressed in writing we began to understand more about the heart of God. He began to reveal himself and show us more about his true desires for us and humanity as a whole. In doing so we realized you can't hope to do God's work without getting an understanding of God the father's motivations. His heart. Why he does what he does and why he wants what he wants. We've clearly established that God's ways are higher than our ways but if our participation is necessary for God to implement his will shouldn't we have some concept of what God's will is? After all, the only thing necessary for God to answer a prayer is that the request be in God's will and a person has the faith to pray for it. Every prayer, every time.

To be honest this chapter was really born out of the first experience we had with going through this book in a group. When we got to the second reflection question of Chapter one regarding how we saw God the Father the answers were astonishing. With few exceptions the entire group of 10+ men described their view of God the Father as an authoritative dictator, anxious to rain down punishment, only to be thwarted by the sacrifice of Jesus Christ. The truly amazing part of this was that many of these men were not new to their walk with Christ. Many were long standing believers who had accepted Christ as their savior many years, if not decades, earlier. These men, who should theoretically have a good, deep grasp of their heavenly father, described a relationship where they timidly approached their heavenly father. They were happy to be saved and certainly recognized the grace inherent in it but saw Jesus as their only heavenly friend. The buddy who knew the bouncer at the nightclub and slipped them in. The ever present intercessor standing at the father's side keeping him from raining down his holy wrath.

Reflection: Go back and review how you answered the second reflection question form Chapter 1. Do you still agree with your assessment of God the Father? Has it changed as you went through the study? Does the answer you gave before still FEEL right?

_____

_____

_____

_____

_____

_____

_____

_____

_____

_____

_____

_____

_____

As we listened to these descriptions our heart broke. **It started to sink in that it's pretty hard to boldly approach the throne of God if we are afraid of the person sitting on it.** We may be saved by faith and have our sins covered but how can we follow a general we don't trust? A father that is anxious to punish us...... Does that sound a little off? God wants to punish sin, he's anxious to rain down wrath? To most of us that FEELS wrong. We know God is perfect and loves us so he obviously wants what's best for us. How does that align with this impression of a heavenly father just itching to punish us. A father of justice. A father full of wrath and judgment? When we start to break down the different purposes of the Trinity we start to see the "negative" traits consolidate around the person of God the Father. It seems we load all the hard to understand, apparently contradictory traits, on the farther but in reality it is revealing many of our true concerns about God. Remember this is three existences of the same being. All one but all separate. These feelings about God the father are really issues with God as a whole. If we are honest about it, that is the ultimate conclusion of a concept of a wrathful father. A God that's hard to trust. A God that is hard to get close to. But that doesn't make sense. God is perfect.

> [48]Be   perfect,   therefore,   as   your
> heavenly Father is perfect.
>
> *Mathew 5:48*

HE IS LOVE.

God is love.

1 John 4:16

....

Those very clear and succinct scriptures seem to be completely contrary to this image of a wrath filled father. It is even more in contrast to the biblical definition of love.

[4]Love is patient, love is kind. It does not envy, it does not boast, it is not proud. [5]It does not dishonor others, it is not self-seeking, it is not easily angered, it keeps no record of wrongs. [6]Love does not delight in evil but rejoices with the truth. [7]It always protects, always trusts, always hopes, always perseveres.

1 Corinthians 13:4-7

....

If that is the case then we must have our vision of the Father wrong. We must not understand the heart of God. The heart is a complicated concept but can be best understood when we start looking at it as the will of God. What a person wants (their will) will always be a reflection of their heart. If the heart is not right then the desires will not be. Our hearts must be a reflection of God's in order for us to pray a faith filled prayer that aligns with him. Let's look at what the scriptures tell us about God's will so that we can start to understand his heart.

GOD DESIRES FOR YOU TO HAVE AN ABUNDANT LIFE.

Jesus said this explicitly in the book of John.

> ¹⁰The thief does not come except to steal, and to kill, and to destroy. I have come that they may have life, and that they may have it more abundantly.
>
> *John 10:10*

The New Living Translation gives this a little more relatable context.

> ¹⁰The thief's purpose is to steal and kill and destroy. My purpose is to give them a rich and satisfying life.
>
> *John 10:10*

God even confirmed this in his promise to the Israelites while in captivity.

> ¹¹For I know the plans I have for you," declares the Lord, "plans to prosper you and not to harm you, plans to give you hope and a future.
>
> *Jeremiah 29:11*

[33]Walk in obedience to all that the Lord your God has commanded you, so that you may live and prosper and prolong your days in the land that you will possess.

Deuteronomy 5:33

Reflection: How about you, do you feel like you are living an abundant life? What constitutes abundance? And do you really believe it is God's will for you to live a life of abundance?

_____

_____

_____

_____

_____

_____

_____

_____

_____

_____

_____

_____

_____

This abundance is not just for our own benefit though. God expects us to use it to further his kingdom. Jesus told a parable about blessing and abundance.

> [14] Again, it will be like a man going on a journey, who called his servants and entrusted his wealth to them. [15]To one he gave five bags of gold, to another two bags, and to another one bag, each according to his ability. Then he went on his journey. [16]The man who had received five bags of gold went at once and put his money to work and gained five bags more. [17]So also, the one with two bags of gold gained two more. [18]But the man who had received one bag went off, dug a hole in the ground and hid his master's money.

> [19]"After a long time the master of those servants returned and settled accounts with them. [20]The man who had received five bags of gold brought the other five. 'Master,' he said, 'you entrusted me with five bags of gold. See, I have gained five more.'

> [21]"His master replied, 'Well done, good and faithful servant! You have been faithful with a few things; I will put you in charge of many things. Come and share your master's happiness!'

> [22]"The man with two bags of gold also came. 'Master,' he said, 'you entrusted me with two bags of gold; see, I have gained two more.'

[23]"His master replied, 'Well done, good and faithful servant! You have been faithful with a few things; I will put you in charge of many things. Come and share your master's happiness!'

[24]"Then the man who had received one bag of gold came. 'Master,' he said, 'I knew that you are a hard man, harvesting where you have not sown and gathering where you have not scattered seed.25So I was afraid and went out and hid your gold in the ground. See, here is what belongs to you.'

[26]"His master replied, 'You wicked, lazy servant! So you knew that I harvest where I have not sown and gather where I have not scattered seed? [27]Well then, you should have put my money on deposit with the bankers, so that when I returned I would have received it back with interest.

[28]" 'So take the bag of gold from him and give it to the one who has ten bags.[29]For whoever has will be given more, and they will have an abundance. Whoever does not have, even what they have will be taken from them.[30]And throw that worthless servant outside, into the darkness, where there will be weeping and gnashing of teeth.'

Matthew 25:14-30

Jesus is clear that each of the servants was gifted according to his ability and each was responsible for what they did with those gifts. The results of the parable for the first two servants is self explanatory but the third seems harsh. He not only lost the gift that was given to him but he was thrown out into the darkness. This seems to be contrary to the grace of God. We are cast out and lose our gift when we fail to use it for him? Perhaps this is because this is a natural system that God created. Remember the analogy of the coach? What would happen if we didn't practice those techniques taught to us? What would happen if we didn't run the play as the coach intended? If we did it mostly his way but changed it to suit our desires? Would we still win? Would we score as many points? Would the game be as fun? Perhaps the answer to this question of harshness is that it isn't the coaches choice to make you lose the gift. Perhaps it's a natural consequence of not using it. Perhaps, the act of using the gift is the very abundance we are seeking.

Paul had a very developed perspective on using the gifts God gave you. We've discussed him earlier but here is a quick recap, he'd been shipwrecked, snake bit, beaten to near death multiple times, chased, harassed, whipped, and ultimately imprisoned. All this while doing the very thing that God asked of him. Theoretically living in God's divine will for his life. What did he have to say?

²⁴However, I consider my life worth nothing to me; my only aim is to finish the race and complete the task the Lord Jesus has given me—the task of testifying to the good news of God's grace.

Acts 20:24

And

¹¹I am not saying this because I am in need, for I have learned to be content whatever the circumstances. ¹²I know what it is to be in need, and I know what it is to have plenty. I have learned the secret of being content in any and every situation, whether well fed or hungry, whether living in plenty or in want. ¹³I can do all this through him who gives me strength.

Philippians 4:11-13

Again we see God's very nature being revealed. God grants those in his will the strength to endure any situation they are in. He is love and his love desires the very best for your life. He is the creator of the world, the designer of the game, and he knows the way to win. He designed it so the joy and abundance he promises comes from the very act of playing the game. When we obey him we are promised to grow closer to the spirit with all the blessings that entails. What are those?

> ²²But the fruit of the Spirit is
> love, joy, peace, forbearance, kindness,
> goodness, faithfulness, ²³gentleness and
> self-control. Against such things there
> is no law.
>
> *Galatians 5:22*

....

That sounds like abundance.

GOD DESIRES RELATIONSHIPS WITH MAN.

The first and clearest component of God's will is his desire for a relationship with man. At first glance it seems odd that the creator of the universe wants a relationship with a person but its very clear that he does. If you go back to man prior to the fall we would presumably see God's intended will for his relationship with us. After all this is how he intended man to interact since they had not yet ate the fruit of the tree of the knowledge of good and evil. You see a situation where it is not uncommon for God to walk among man and Adam and Eve both had an opportunity to physically interact with him. This can be clearly seen in the Genesis following the original sin.

> ⁸Then the man and his wife heard the
> sound of the LordGod as he was walking in
> the garden in the cool of the day, and
> they hid from the LordGod among the trees
> of the garden. ⁹But the LordGod called to
> the man, "Where are you?" ¹⁰He answered,
> "I heard you in the garden, and I was
> afraid because I was naked; so I hid."
> ¹¹And he said, "Who told you that you were

naked? Have you eaten from the tree that
I commanded you not to eat from?" ¹²The
man said, "The woman you put here with
me—she gave me some fruit from the tree,
and I ate it." ¹³Then the LordGod said to
the woman, "What is this you have done?"
The woman said, "The serpent deceived me,
and I ate."

Genesis 3:8-13

We can tell that it was not uncommon for God to "walk in the garden" and they were able to personally converse with God. We can see a much more familiar and informal relationship with the father than we enjoy today. Presumably this is what the Father desires. After the fall you then see a series of covenants that God enters into with man.

A COVENANT WITH NOAH

This was the first covenant recorded between man and God. This one is pretty straight forward in that God says he will never destroy the world by flood again. It's interesting to note this covenant immediately follows God affirming Noah's descendants (all of mankind) dominion over the earth.

⁸Then God said to Noah and to his sons
with him: ⁹"I now establish my covenant
with you and with your descendants after
you ¹⁰and with every living creature that
was with you—the birds, the livestock
and all the wild animals, all those
that came out of the ark with you—every

living creature on earth. [11]I establish
my covenant with you: Never again will
all life be destroyed by the waters of a
flood; never again will there be a flood to
destroy the earth."

Genesis 9:8-11

Reflection: Take a moment and look at the flood from God's perspective. What do you see? A hysterically laughing dictator? A proud, vengeful being, glad we got what we deserve? Maybe you see a hurting and sobbing creator wishing, between gasps, that it didn't have to be this way? Is it something else that you see?

_____

_____

_____

_____

_____

_____

_____

_____

_____

_____

_____

_____

_____

_____

A COVENANT WITH ABRAHAM

The covenant with Abraham is the next covenant you see God enter into. When God entered into a covenant with Abraham (then Abram) he assured him he would make him a great nation and "all the peoples of the earth will be blessed through him". God refines this covenant with Abram several times with the wording and commitment from the lord becoming more committed, specific, and intense with each show of obedience by Abraham.

> ²"I will make you into a great nation, and I will bless you; I will make your name great, and you will be a blessing. ³I will bless those who bless you, and whoever curses you I will curse; and all peoples on earth will be blessed through you."
>
> *Genesis 12:2-3*

A COVENANT WITH MOSES (AND ALL OF ISRAEL)

The covenant with Moses is where the stipulations on man start getting more complicated. In this covenant God promises to make Israel his treasured possession and to live among them. In order for this to be fulfilled he gave them the 10 commandments and the law of Moses. This is where all the Jewish rules, like not eating pork or working on the sabbath originated. This is also the first time that God begins to dwell among man again post flood.

³Then Moses went up to God, and the Lord called to him from the mountain and said, "This is what you are to say to the descendants of Jacob and what you are to tell the people of Israel: ⁴'You yourselves have seen what I did to Egypt, and how I carried you on eagles' wings and brought you to myself. ⁵Now if you obey me fully and keep my covenant, then out of all nations you will be my treasured possession. Although the whole earth is mine, ⁶you will be for me a kingdom of priests and a holy nation.' These are the words you are to speak to the Israelites."

⁷So Moses went back and summoned the elders of the people and set before them all the words the Lord had commanded him to speak. ⁸The people all responded together, "We will do everything the Lord has said." So Moses brought their answer back to the Lord.

Exodus 19:3-8

....

⁴²"For the generations to come this burnt offering is to be made regularly at the entrance to the tent of meeting, before the Lord. There I will meet you and speak to you; ⁴³there also I will meet with the Israelites, and the place will be consecrated by my glory.

⁴⁴"So I will consecrate the tent of meeting and the altar and will consecrate Aaron and his sons to serve me as priests. ⁴⁵Then I will dwell among the Israelites and be their God. ⁴⁶They will know that I

am the Lord their God, who brought them
out of Egypt so that I might dwell among
them. I am the Lord their God.

Exodus 29-42-46

....

A COVENANT WITH DAVID

The covenant with David is where things begin to change. In this covenant God promises that David's lineage will forever be on the throne. God frequently confirms this covenant to David's descendants but always does so for the "benefit of my servant David".

"The Lord declares to you that the
Lord himself will establish a house for
you: [12]When your days are over and you
rest with your ancestors, I will raise up
your offspring to succeed you, your own
flesh and blood, and I will establish his
kingdom. [13]He is the one who will build a
house for my Name, and I will establish
the throne of his kingdom forever. [14]I
will be his father, and he will be my son.
When he does wrong, I will punish him
with a rod wielded by men, with floggings
inflicted by human hands. [15]But my love
will never be taken away from him, as I
took it away from Saul, whom I removed
from before you. [16]Your house and your
kingdom will endure forever before me;
your throne will be established forever."

2 Samuel 7:11-16

....

A NEW COVENANT

This covenant is described in the book of Jeremiah as the words of God to Jeremiah in a dream.

> ³¹"The days are coming," declares the Lord, "when I will make a new covenant with the people of Israel and with the people of Judah. ³²It will not be like the covenant I made with their ancestors when I took them by the hand to lead them out of Egypt, because they broke my covenant, though I was a husband to them," declares the Lord. ³³"This is the covenant I will make with the people of Israel after that time," declares the Lord. "I will put my law in their minds and write it on their hearts. I will be their God, and they will be my people. ³⁴No longer will they teach their neighbor, or say to one another, 'Know the Lord,' because they will all know me, from the least of them to the greatest," declares the Lord. "For I will forgive their wickedness and will remember their sins no more."

Jeremiah 31:31-34

This is the final unconditional covenant between God and man spoke about in the bible. This covenant is a foreshadowing of the coming of Christ and his sacrifice reconciling man to God. The final correction of the relationship between man & God. This is confirmed in the new testament when the writer of Hebrews discussed the scripture from Jeremiah.

> ¹³By calling this covenant "new,"
> he has made the first one obsolete; and
> what is obsolete and outdated will soon
> disappear.

Hebrews 8:13

It's important that we have this in the correct context. If you go back and look at the substance of each of the covenants you'll note a softening of God at each iteration. You'll also note that God draws himself closer to man with each iteration. Hundreds if not thousands of years of history just to create a time when he could send his Son so we might be made right with him. How does that align with the image of an angry vengeful God? How can a God that literally designed and implemented a several hundred year plan involving generations of intentional steps be anxious to punish you?

Perhaps that leads to the next logical question: Why did it take so long for God to implement this solution? Couldn't he have just sent Jesus as soon as the fall in the garden of Eden? To answer that question, let's look at each of the major unconditioned covenants again.

NOAH

I will never destroy the earth by flood again. This represents God committing to bring man back to him. He won't just wipe them out and start over. This seems insignificant but it is a major move of God. Up to this point God had been letting man run down the road they had chosen. Sin and lawlessness abound. The world is hopelessly corrupted and is not making any attempt to turn back to the relationship with him. The rotten seed had been planted and up to the point of the flood, God was just letting it play out. We had not yet reached full corruption. The world was on the downhill slide and had to hit bottom in order to start climbing the hill again. Much like many of us we had to hit a bottom of our own pride, selfishness, or give in deeply to temptation before we ever realized we needed a savior. We couldn't do it on our own.

ABRAHAM

I will make a holy priesthood and a chosen people from you. This is the beginning of God "fixing" the relationship. Again why did it take so long? Let's look at what he told Abraham when he renewed the covenant with him.

> [12]As the sun was setting, Abram fell into a deep sleep, and a thick and dreadful darkness came over him. [13]Then the Lord said to him, "Know for certain that for four hundred years your descendants will be strangers in a country not their own and that they will be enslaved and mistreated there. [14]But I will punish the nation they serve as slaves, and afterward they will come out with great possessions. [15]You, however, will go to your ancestors in peace and be buried at a good old age. [16]In the fourth generation your descendants will come back here, for the sin of the Amorites has not yet reached its full measure."
>
> *Genesis 15:12-16*

Again we can see it is actually God's grace that is keeping him from jumping right into the next covenant. The people the Israelites would need to kill in order to receive the promised land had not yet earned that judgment from God. Apparently, they needed 400 years more of a downhill slide before justice could be satisfied with their death.

MOSES

The covenant of the Law. At this point God chooses a people and actually begins to dwell among man again. He physically occupies the temple and speaks directly to the entire people of Israel at one point. But again, this is imperfect. His very presence hurts them. He can't really get close to them because of his perfect nature. He can't have a true relationship because of their unpaid sin. That is one of the reasons for the constant sacrifices. They need those just to have the limited relationship that they had with God. So why go through this step at all? That answer can be seen in the new testament.

> [20]The law was brought in so that the trespass might increase. But where sin increased, grace increased all the more,
>
> *Romans 5:20*

> ²⁷God did this so that they would seek
> him and perhaps reach out for him and find
> him, though he is not far from any one
> of us.

Acts 17:27

....

You see, in the light of the sacrifice made by Jesus, the reason for those old testament covenants becomes clear. We needed the covenant of the Law so that it was clear what Jesus was doing. It showed how dirty we were and that there was no way we could get clean through our own works. It gave us a way to "measure" our sin.

DAVID

A promise that a new dynasty is born. This is where God promises a solution to the relationship problem. David didn't understand it at the time but this covenant was a commitment to bring Jesus to earth via his lineage. A promise to fix the problem created in Eden. A promise to reunite man and God.

This was confirmed by the angel Gabriel:

> ³⁰But the angel said to her, "Do not be
> afraid, Mary; you have found favor with
> God. ³¹You will conceive and give birth to
> a son, and you are to call him Jesus. ³²He
> will be great and will be called the Son
> of the Most High. The Lord God will give
> him the throne of his father David, ³³and
> he will reign over Jacob's descendants
> forever; his kingdom will never end."

Luke 1:30-33

....

JESUS

The new covenant. Man made clean and able to dwell with God. The end game. Or is it? In reality it is not God's final solution, it is a path to that solution. It still requires action on our part but it gives us an ability to take that action. We aren't clean just because Jesus died, we are clean because we accept that sacrifice and choose to follow him. We have an option to choose again. Finally the Garden of Eden reborn. Man with a choice to dwell with God or not.

Let's use an analogy for this process. Let's say that God's relationship with man is dinner. When Adam and Eve chose to eat from the tree they didn't just leave the table, they destroyed it. God no longer had a place to eat with man. The covenant with Noah was God writing an invitation to a new dinner party. The covenant with Abraham built a new table but unfortunately it didn't come with any chairs. The covenant with Moses gave us a plan for chairs but we don't have the expertise necessary to build them. God promises David's lineage will provide someone to build the chairs, a carpenter. Finally Christ follows God's will to the cross thereby building the chairs. Now all that we need to do is choose to sit in our chair and have dinner with God.

That explanation may make God's process reasonable but what about all those people that existed between Adam and Jesus. Are they left with no way to reconcile with God? God apparently solved for them as well.

> ⁵⁰Then Jesus shouted out again, and he released his spirit. ⁵¹At that moment the curtain in the sanctuary of the Temple was torn in two, from top to bottom. The earth shook, rocks split apart, ⁵²and tombs opened. The bodies of many godly men and women who had died were raised from the dead. ⁵³They left the cemetery after Jesus' resurrection, went into the holy city of Jerusalem, and appeared to many people.
>
> *Mathew 27 50-53 NLT*

We have to remember that God gave us a choice to sin because without a choice it isn't really love. We then chose to sin and walk away from that relationship with God. This wasn't a small problem, this was a major violation of the relationship. Love requires a choice and we chose not to love him. We chose to ignore his perfect path and make one for ourselves. We chose to not live with God. Correcting this choice without taking away the right to make a choice was complicated and took hundreds of years for God to accomplish.

That picture of God, a picture of a loving father working diligently for hundreds of years just to get back to his kids, begins to put the scripture from Peter in a little clearer light.

> The Lord is not slow in keeping his
> promise, as some understand slowness.
> Instead he is patient with you, not
> wanting anyone to perish, but everyone
> to come to repentance.

2 Peter 3:9

....

We must remember that God experiences yesterday, today, and tomorrow all at the same time. He is not confined by space or time. A decision made today plays out instantly to him. He is not slow, he is patient, he is perfect. God wanted to return to a relationship with EVERYONE of his children. A big mistake takes a big plan to bring reconciliation and that is what God did. He had to let us experience the natural consequence of our choice but still wanted to protect us from an eternity without him. He needed a plan that let us still make the choice but still satisfied his nature which demands justice. He had to let us choose him. He had to be true to his nature. He had to be love.

> [10]This is love: not that we loved God,
> but that he loved us and sent his Son as
> an atoning sacrifice for our sins

1 John 4:10

....

Reflection: Now, presented with this new perspective of the journey back to the presence of God, his perfect plan to reunite us with him, does it change the way you view his actions from the old testament? Does it begin to heal the paradox inside of us that says God is jealous, God is vengeful, God kills people and God is patient, God is kind, God is love? Can you see God's heart now?

_____

_____

_____

_____

_____

_____

_____

_____

_____

_____

_____

_____

_____

_____

The last and most clear indication of God the Father's heart comes from one of the most memorized scriptures.

> 16For God so loved the world that he gave his one and only Son, that whoever believes in him shall not perish but have eternal life.
>
> *John 3:16*

This scripture is classic. It clearly demonstrates Jesus loved us so much he died for us on the cross...right? If you look more closely that isn't actually what it says. What else does scripture tell us about Jesus and the cross?

> 8And being found in appearance as a man, he humbled himself by becoming obedient to death—even death on a cross!
>
> *Phillipians 2:8*

Combine those two scriptures and we see that it wasn't Jesus' love for us that put him on the cross. It was Jesus' obedience to the Father that put him on the cross and God's love for us that required it. That's a perspective shift if you let it set in. Jesus went to the cross because his father told him to but it was the immense and immeasurable love for us that led that same father to ask him to do it! Does that sound like a God of wrath?

To close out this book it seems appropriate to blend a couple of scriptures that we have already used.

1 John 4:16 says God is love and 1 Corinthians 13:4-7 says what love is. If we combine the two we find out God's own description of his heart.

God is patient, God is kind. He does not envy, he does not boast, he is not proud. He does not dishonor others, he is not self-seeking, he is not easily angered, he keeps no record of wrongs. God does not delight in evil but rejoices with the truth. He always protects, always trusts, always hopes, always perseveres.

When we attempt to understand God's actions or desires we must attempt to view it from God's point of view. Filter it through his lense. If you look at any of the above statements and say that doesn't align with XXXX scripture or YYYY statement, dig deeper. Are you looking at an instant that is in the middle of an incredibly complicated plan involving choice and justice? Is there maybe a different motive that you didn't consider that is more subtle but conforms to the above statement?

Reread the above blended scripture. He keeps no record of wrongs...does that sound like a God who is anxious to punish? He is patient and kind ...does that sound like someone who is ready to rain down wrath? He is not self-seeking...does that sound like a God who wants to control what you do and say? When we look at his self description does it sound like a wise, loving father who is anxious to teach you how to play the game of life? Who hopes you will learn and listen and become a star athlete. Who desires to talk with you and hear you problems.

Who wants nothing more than to see you live the best possible existence. This is the heart of God...to love you... to walk with you...to prosper you...and to complete you.

GOD IS LOVE.